MAN UP

Recapturing the Heart of Manhood

Jason Hanash

Renown Publishing
www.renownpublishing.com

Man Up / Jason Hanash
ISBN-13: 978-1-952602-76-4

Jason Hanash's book, *Man Up: Recapturing the Heart of Manhood*, does a masterful job in sifting through the commonly held misconceptions about what it means to be a man in today's fluctuating culture—to fully "man up" in life. He frames his succinct purpose to help Christian men "develop a healthy understanding of their God-given identity" with "a vision for their masculinity." Drawing on his seasoned pastoral leadership and passion for ministry to men, he offers a solid, biblically-based framework of understanding God as Father and its implications for men through the stages of their lifelong journey.

Especially vital is his look at the life of David—with all his flaws and strengths—in chapters detailing important aspects of his character as a model for men. Scripturally sound with practical implications for living in reality, this volume is chock full of valuable insights and workbook pages for reflection, which can be read by individual men or, perhaps most helpfully, used for a men's group study in our churches. Toward this end, he sums it up: "So above all, have a heart for God and, in turn, be a man after His heart."

Rich Guerra, SoCal Network Superintendent

Who better to teach us how to *Man Up* than David? I loved Jason's treatment of the guy who was so messed up, but still got the label "a man after God's own heart." Too bad Solomon didn't follow his example. Solomon became unteachable and untouchable and too smart to *Man Up*. Not so with David. All throughout his life, he kept going back to God and allowed the prophets of God to speak into his life. If you want to recapture the heart of a real man, go on this journey with Jason Hanash. I did it and am better for it.

Mike D. Robertson, Author of *Dealing With Difficult People*

Our world desperately needs men who exemplify biblical masculinity. This book will help men to escape the cultural web of lies about what men should be and how they should act, and also to discover God's greater purpose and way of living!

Ryan Visconti, Lead Pastor of Generation Church

Jason Hanash's book, *Man Up: Recapturing the Heart of Manhood*, does a masterful job in sifting through the commonly held misconceptions about what it means to be a man in today's fluctuating culture—to fully "man up" in life. He frames his succinct purpose to help Christian men "develop a healthy understanding of their God-given identity" with "a vision for their masculinity." Drawing on his seasoned pastoral leadership and passion for ministry to men, he offers a solid, biblically-based framework of understanding God as Father and its implications for men through the stages of their lifelong journey.

Especially vital is his look at the life of David—with all his flaws and strengths—in chapters detailing important aspects of his character as a model for men. Scripturally sound with practical implications for living in reality, this volume is chock full of valuable insights and workbook pages for reflection, which can be read by individual men or, perhaps most helpfully, used for a men's group study in our churches. Toward this end, he sums it up: "So above all, have a heart for God and, in turn, be a man after His heart."

Rich Guerra, SoCal Network Superintendent

Who better to teach us how to *Man Up* than David? I loved Jason's treatment of the guy who was so messed up, but still got the label "a man after God's own heart." Too bad Solomon didn't follow his example. Solomon became unteachable and untouchable and too smart to *Man Up*. Not so with David. All throughout his life, he kept going back to God and allowed the prophets of God to speak into his life. If you want to recapture the heart of a real man, go on this journey with Jason Hanash. I did it and am better for it.

Mike D. Robertson, Author of *Dealing With Difficult People*

Our world desperately needs men who exemplify biblical masculinity. This book will help men to escape the cultural web of lies about what men should be and how they should act, and also to discover God's greater purpose and way of living!

Ryan Visconti, Lead Pastor of Generation Church

To the man who didn't have a man to show him the way.

May this book help you on the journey to authentic manhood.

CONTENTS

Foreword
by Chris Sonksen

Success outside the home never compensates for failure within it. This is a rallying cry that I have been promoting to men throughout my many years of ministry. You can climb the corporate ladder, develop a highly successful business, or obtain a certain level of financial status, but it will never compensate for failure inside of the home. America has never lacked for innovators or entrepreneurs, but our nation has desperately lacked for men who will lead their family, love their wife, and live a life worth following. As the founding pastor of South Hills Church, a multi-site ministry, and the founder of Church Boom, an organization that coaches pastors and leaders, I have seen first-hand the devastation of men who have failed to lead their family or even to lead their own life.

That is why I am so excited for the timely and much-needed book, *Man Up!* It is written by my friend and partner in kingdom work, Jason Hanash. I have been honored to have a front-row seat to this man's life and ministry. His public status as the lead pastor of Discovery Church is remarkable. I was part of the conversations when this church first started, and I have seen it flourish into one of the fastest-growing churches in America. Each step of the journey, Jason has led the church with courage and integrity.

However, his greatest accomplishment doesn't lie inside the four walls of Discovery. His biggest achievement is his role as both father and husband. He has fostered a wonderful relationship with his wife, Veronica, and has excelled in leading and guiding his children. He has woven together in all his relationships a spirit of love, faith, gentleness, courage, and character. Jason didn't just write *Man Up*—he lives *Man Up!*

As you read through the pages of this incredible book, you will find practical and biblical insights that will challenge you to redefine manhood. It speaks to the spirit and soul of every many who is brave enough to explore this book with an open heart and who is willing to apply the life-changing principles that leap from the pages. There are so many nuggets of truth filling each chapter, it's hard to pick out just a few. However, as I personally read through the chapters, I discovered two driving themes. These overarching principles set not only a foundation for this book but also a foundation for your life.

The first driving theme you'll discover is a new understanding of God's idea of manhood. For years, society has painted a false concept of what manhood is and is not. Clearly, this picture hasn't led us to stronger families and greater men. God, however, has a very clear idea of manhood, which only makes sense: his idea would be the right one since he is the one who created man.

The second driving theme centers on the wounds and scars that many men carry throughout their life. These pain points often come from our upbringing and experiences that we had as children, teenagers, or even adults. Maybe you had a father who abandoned you or who never really modeled true manhood in front of you. Maybe you never felt loved or accepted by your father, so you find it difficult to know how to show love to the people in your life. Or possibly, you never felt encouraged by your father, so you have lived a life believing that you weren't good enough or strong enough to become who you were meant to be. *Man Up* explores these sacred areas of our lives and creates a pathway that leads us to greater understanding of God's clear idea of manhood.

Every once in a while, a book comes along that can redefine a generation and reshape our culture. *Man Up* is one of those books! It is more than simply words on a page; it reflects the heart of our loving Father. It gives us insight into what God wants to breathe into each of us as men. This is not simply a foreword from me, or even an endorsement. It is a plea for you to read every page of this book and let it do what it was meant to do: change your life! Trust me as a leader, pastor, and friend when I say this book has the ability to revolutionize who you are and who you are becoming.

The book of Genesis states all the things that God created: the stars, moon, sun, plants, mountains, trees, ocean, and every other magnificent thing we find in this world. In each case, the Bible declares that God spoke it into existence.

Whether it was with a tree or a star, he spoke and nothing became something. What's interesting is that when God created man, it doesn't say that he spoke it into existence; instead, it says, he breathed into man (Genesis 2:7). We as men weren't spoken into existence, but the creator of this universe breathed into us. We have his air in our lungs; he gave us our first breath. Because of this, we were created in his image.

We've allowed our past and sometimes even our present to shape the men we have become. We have drifted away from the ultimate model of manhood, which is our amazing and powerful God. So, I challenge you to lean in and listen closely. If you quiet your heart, you will hear a still, small voice calling your name. It's the voice of our God, who with the same breath that breathed you into existence is breathing these words to you right now: *It's time to Man Up!*

INTRODUCTION

The Unfinished Man

What does it mean to be a man?

Too many people today are confused about masculinity and manhood, caught up in popular misunderstandings and deceptions. Our culture has reframed identity and gender, including masculinity, to the point that even believers have a tough time comprehending what it means to be a man, particularly a man following Jesus.

To some people today, being a man is an identity based in how they feel.

To others, it's about being hyper-aggressive or dominating other people, whether physically, with money, or with other kinds of power our culture respects.

And on the flip side, we now encounter the cultural bias that's hostile to, or at least suspicious of, any positive discussion about what it means to be a man. It's the attitude that assumes if you're affirming any kind of masculinity, you're just trying to put sheep's clothing on the domineering, destructive wolf of "toxic masculinity."

Again, Christians aren't immune from any of this confusion. So many followers of Jesus are unsure or unaware of what it means, biblically, to man up. Our world is in critical condition, and we need men to develop a healthy understanding of their God-given identity.

Over my years in leadership and ministry, God has given me a passion to address this current reality in the lives of men. That's why I helped start an intentional mentorship program called Brotherhood for men at my church; it's also the reason for the book you're reading now. Men need a vision for their masculinity.

So, let's return to the original question, revising it slightly: in God's view—biblically—*what does it mean to be man?*

The answer hinges on understanding the character of our heavenly Father, which also affects how we fill our roles as fathers. To become who God calls him to be, every man needs a relationship with his Father in heaven. That's where real manhood begins, without exception.

What do we know about the character of our heavenly Father? Well, the best place to start is Jesus, who perfectly exemplified the character of the Father for us. It's the Lord's desire that men and women should exemplify His character as well, the way Jesus showed us. But for men, I've found that the aspect of God's character with which we struggle most, the biggest missing piece, is with God as Father.

In this book, I want to help address the gap in our understanding of fatherhood. That said, the message and contents of these chapters touch on every aspect of a man's journey, from the adventures of young adulthood to our work passing the torch to the next generation. Brotherhood and friendship, mission and purpose, passion and love, and leadership all play a part. But let's be honest: men also experience seasons of failure and loss, and we often have lingering wounds from our relationship with our earthly father. We'll look at those difficult realities of being a man, too.

SIX STAGES OF MASCULINITY

What it means to be a man varies depending on our stage of life. I've found it useful to talk about masculinity in terms of the six stages John Eldredge describes in his book, *Fathered by God.*[1] Keep in mind that there is some overlap: some features of one stage can be found in the others. Even though these transformations aren't always obvious, or the same for everyone, they can help us better appreciate what it means to man up in the kingdom of God.

Each of the six stages presents its own set of obstacles and insights related to the process of becoming a man. But one of the most important truths to take away from all of these stages, Eldredge points out, is that a child can only become a man via his father's active involvement and the fellowship of other men. It's not going to happen any other way.

Let me begin by describing the six stages of masculinity:

Boyhood

We have a natural desire for a father's affection and

approval, which signal to a boy that he is valued and adored. Boyhood is the stage when we want to be the favored son, the apple of our father's eye. It should be a time of affirmation for a son as a person—when we experience our father's unconditional love, through which we learn about our heavenly Father's love.

The Cowboy

Young men normally start their cowboy period at the age of thirteen, when they enter puberty. In biblical culture, this might have been called the shepherd phase, because contrary to popular imagination today, shepherds lived a grungy, rugged existence on the periphery of society, similar to cowboys in the modern era. No matter what we call it, this part of a man's life usually lasts from his adolescence to his early twenties. It's a period when he's out in the field absorbing life lessons.

Every man asks himself the same question: "Do I have what it takes?" Do we have what it takes to be men? To be husbands and fathers—to lead our families? We tend to push limits and learn lessons the hard way when we're in the cowboy stage. It's a time for adventure, testing, hard work, and discovering whether or not we have what is required to survive and prosper in the world.

Perhaps a man will learn to score touchdowns or throw curve balls during this time in his life. He'll almost certainly obtain his first car, which will expand his horizons. Maybe he'll go on solitary expeditions, or maybe he'll go with a group of friends, bonding with other young men over the dangers they take, the losses they face, and the victories they achieve.

The Warrior

Sometime in a young man's late teens, typically, the warrior comes to the fore. Now, remember I said that these stages overlap. A man will always be a warrior, whether he is six or sixty years old, since he bears the image of a warrior God.

Passivity and masculinity are essentially opposed.

However, by our late teens and twenties, the warrior component of our personality tends to take center stage in our lives. Anyone who believes that this is antiquated, violent, or even primitive should understand, passivity and masculinity are essentially opposed. We must live with courage and discipline, which frequently necessitates action and battle.

But for what reason? What steps are we going to take? What kinds of wars do we engage in? The warrior requires guidance, which can only be provided by having a cause and a king (leader). It's critical for a warrior to have a mission—a defined goal—and, more importantly, to understand how to spiritually battle the kingdom of darkness.

This stage may cause a man to enlist in the military and become an actual warrior. Or he may become a teacher, battling for young people's hearts and minds. He could put his skills to the test in a trade, at a small firm, or in the corporate sector. Regardless of our individual path as a warrior, if God is our High King, we will know the conflicts we must fight and will have the fortitude to do so.

The Lover

And it's during this period, when a man is in his late teens or early twenties, that he also becomes the lover. Now, it would be best for him, as well as for any woman in his life, if he lived as a warrior for a while. Too many young cowboys don't get their questions answered, leaving them as unsure warriors with no mission in life. They end up bringing all of their uncertainty into their love connection, in the hopes of finding affirmation and a reason to live in a woman. A lover, on the other hand, comes to give strength to a woman, not to take it away.

The lover stage entails discovering the way of our hearts as men, in addition to the importance of a relationship with a woman. Our spiritual lives reach new heights. We realize that poetry and passion can be more reliable guides to truth than logic and reason. We become more aware of life's beauty, including music and literature.

Man as lover, like King David in the Bible, becomes a romantic, elevating his spiritual life to new heights. This stage is all about passion and depth of heart, which help a man grow closer to God. As a warrior, service to God is still crucial, but obedience born of the intimacy of his relationship with his heavenly Father now triumphs over what previously could have been a reflexive or logical obedience to God as a distant King or abstract Cause.

What we now have is a world where largely boys are going about in men's bodies, with jobs, families, income, and other obligations that belong to men.

A man can only become a king or a leader if he has this level of relationship with the Lord and appreciation for beauty.

The King

The hard truth that men have been given power but are unprepared to handle it is at the heart of our world's current crises, from business and politics to the church and the home. What we now have is a world where, largely, boys are going about in men's bodies, with jobs, families, income, and other obligations that belong to men.

There is a measure of incompleteness inside our soul that causes us to reach outside of God's design to grab hold of things not intended for us.

Though each stage of masculinity provides Christian men with opportunities to learn various lessons, any one of these stages can be injured or cut short, leaving the growing man with an underdeveloped, immature soul in some ways. We learn we are incomplete men in these situations, and only God can complete us.

For example, a man experiencing a midlife crisis is frequently a result of him gaining money and power and then utilizing it to try to make up for unfinished business from prior phases. To make up for lost boyhood memories as a loving son, he would purchase himself toys, such as an expensive automobile or boat. Or he might embark on trips in search of whatever he believes he was missing during his cowboy days. There is a measure of incompleteness inside our soul that causes us to reach outside of God's design to grab hold of things not intended for us.

And these vain attempts to find fulfillment apart from God leave us unfinished. The ways in which we are unfinished men undercut us and, at times, knock us down— seemingly out of nowhere, like a tree downed in the yard after a night of high winds. On closer investigation, the tree might have roots that failed to attach it firmly enough in the dirt. Maybe drought and disease had rotted it from the inside. The inner lives of many men today are likewise poorly rooted and malnourished.

I don't know where you are unfinished. I know where I was unfinished: I was raised without a father in my home, and my mother was not present, attentive, or intentional. Growing up, I did not receive the affirmation or love I needed. That's where the Lord had to bring healing and make me whole.

We are imperfect; our fathers were imperfect. However, true leadership and responsibility require men to be prepared and ready. The time of rule is a severe test of character, and we won't be able to endure the strong winds if we aren't firmly established in our relationship with God.

The Sage

As a man's years pass, his jurisdiction may get smaller. If he has children, they will ultimately depart, so he may need to downsize. His salary may diminish, but his influence is expected to rise.

When some men believe their time has passed, they may be on the verge of making their most significant contributions to God's kingdom.

This isn't the time to pack our belongings and relocate to a warmer climate to pass the time. We don't have license to retire early from a life of duty, discipline, and bearing fruit for God's kingdom, even if we retire from our occupations at some point. Our mission does not come to an end on some random birthday.

The kingdom needs men to serve as sages, who are the elders and gatekeepers. Their goal is to pass on their hard-won, God-given knowledge to the next generation. When some men believe their time has passed, they may be on the verge of making their most significant contributions to God's kingdom. In His kingdom, weakness is an opportunity to rely on God for strength. So, as our physical strength and vitality wane in old age, God can use us powerfully to shape the people around us with His wisdom and our life experience.

We see these stages of masculinity, and some shortcomings in living up to God's ideals for manhood, in the biblical account of David. In the chapters that follow, we'll look at

King David's life as an illustration of what it means to be a man, on God's terms—and as an example of the realities of temptation and failure. We pick up his story in 1 Samuel 16, where he is a young man in the cowboy stage (for him, literally, the shepherd stage). From there, we can follow his life story through the books of 1 and 2 Samuel and into the first couple chapters of 1 Kings. David made his reputation as a warrior and a king, but he was also a lover and a sage.

As you read this book, think about the ways the stages of masculinity shaped David's life. Think also about the ways in which David might have been an unfinished man, based on the biblical accounts. Beyond that, however, I encourage you to reflect on the stages you've already experienced personally and on whatever stage(s) you're at currently. My hope is that this book will affirm you in recapturing the heart of manhood, pursuing healthy masculinity at every stage in life, by growing closer to your Father in heaven like David sought to do. Becoming a man after God's heart begins and ends with Him.

A Man After God's Heart

*But God removed Saul and replaced him with David, a man about whom God said, "I have found David son of Jesse, **a man after my own heart**. He will do everything I want him to do."*

—***Acts 13:22***

Fourteen chapters of the book of Genesis are devoted to the life of Abraham.

Fourteen chapters later in Genesis recount the story of Joseph.

The life of Elijah features in ten chapters across the books of 1 and 2 Kings.

Each of these men also receives mention in other books of the Old and New Testaments.

But none of these people—in fact, no one else besides Jesus—gets as much attention in the Bible as David. Sixty-six chapters of the Bible tell the story of his life and his reign as king. The books of 1 and 2 Samuel and 1 and 2 Chronicles focus heavily on David, and biblical writers mentioned his name nearly one thousand times in all, across the Old and New Testaments.[2] David himself composed much of the book of Psalms. Clearly, he was a guy God wanted us to know about. But, why?

Though David was a flawed man who made many mistakes and committed sins, he was God's chosen king of Israel. More importantly, David was a man after God's own heart (1 Samuel 13:14, Acts 13:22). Generations later, God would send His one and only Son, Jesus, whose earthly lineage descended from David, to reign on the throne of David as the King of kings and Lord of lords.

A MAN AFTER GOD'S HEART— WHAT IT'S NOT

What does it mean to be a man after God's own heart? From 1 Samuel 13:14, which contrasts young David with King Saul, we know that keeping the Lord's commands is part of it. But as we seek to understand God's description of David's character more fully, let's start by identifying what it *doesn't* mean.

It's Not Perfection

Being a man after God's heart does not mean you never make mistakes. When God wanted to capture David's whole life and character with a one-liner, He didn't pick the obvious: "David, the great king," or "David, the musician." Nor did He use the unflattering alternatives: "David, the adulterer," or "David, the murderer." It's no coincidence that God summed up David as "a man after my own heart."

Of course, that's great news for you and me, because none of us is perfect—not even close. Yet God makes it clear that whatever you've done in your past doesn't have to be the one-liner that describes you.

You will never see God do great things

if you don't do hard things.

When God scans the earth looking for potential leaders, He is not on a search for angels in the flesh. He is certainly not looking for perfect people, because those don't exist. But He *is* looking for people who share certain qualities He found in David, which He called being a man after His heart.

By the way, yes, all of this applies to being a woman after God's own heart, too!

It's Not Floating on the Clouds

Imagine someone with no problems, no trials, no stress, and no pressure. You know what I call that? It's not being a man after God's heart; I call it being someone in pursuit of comfort. It's someone who never steps out onto the battlefield to fight giants. In other words, it's someone who will never see God do great things because he doesn't want to man up and do the hard things.

Being a man after God's heart is not trial-free or pressure-free. It doesn't try to avoid difficulties, because it's not disconnected from reality; problems are a part of living in the real world! The difference is, a man after God's heart steps onto the battlefields of life at His direction, with confidence that comes from trusting the Lord with the outcome.

It's Not Being Born That Way

Sure, some men seem to have natural talents for leadership, but ultimately, leaders are made, not born. David had to grow into being a man, and a king, after God's own heart. He had to learn how to set his affection and his focus on the Lord, saying, "Lead me by your truth and teach me, for you are the God who saves me. All day long I put my hope in you" (Psalm 25:5). If we put our hope in the Lord, it means we're not trusting in our bank accounts, in the protection of worldly weapons, or in our friends and our social media followers.

But let's start at the beginning: why did Israel need a king? After all, God was their King.

Finally, all the elders of Israel met at Ramah to discuss the matter with Samuel. "Look," they told him, "you are now old, and your sons are not like you. Give us a king to judge us like all the other nations have."
—1 Samuel 8:4-5

The people of Israel were discontent and wanted a human king because they wanted to be like their neighboring nations. It's a dangerous thing to want to be like someone else. Yes, God can teach us how to be men through others who serve as role models and teachers. But don't crave being like everyone (or anyone) else, especially when doing so would compromise the integrity of your faith or your testimony to the truth of the gospel. It's a dangerous thing to want what other people have. The power of biblical masculinity lies with being who God called *you* to be.

Samuel knew as much, and since he was God's prophet, he was probably offended at the people's request, too:

> *Samuel was displeased with their request and went to the*
> *LORD for guidance. "Do everything they say to you," the*
> *LORD replied, "for **they are rejecting me**, not you."*
> **—1 Samuel 8:6–7**

It seems like the Israelites had forgotten about God liberating their forefathers from slavery in Egypt, including how He allowed Moses to part the waters of the Red Sea to help them escape (Exodus 14). They'd apparently forgotten about how God brought down Jericho's walls for them (Joshua 6). and they'd forgotten about the day God made the sun stand still so Joshua and the Israelite army could thoroughly defeat the Amorites (Joshua 10:12–14). God did all of that for His people; yet, they kept forgetting the past, and they failed to trust Him for the future.

*Ever since I brought them from Egypt they have continually abandoned me and followed other gods. And now they are giving you the same treatment. Do as they ask, but solemnly **warn them about the way a king will reign over them.***

—*1 Samuel 8:8–9*

In this situation, God handed the Israelites a severe judgment: He gave them what they wanted. Oftentimes, the worst thing that can happen is to get what we (think we) want. This is why, as men and as leaders, we need to learn to stop praying, "Lord, give me my desire for finding the job I want, the wife I want, and the lifestyle I want," and instead pray, "Lord, give me what You desire for my life. What You want for me is way more important than what I want for me."

When God instructed Samuel to warn the Israelites "about the way a king will reign over them," He meant that the Israelites ought to know what they were in for. A king wasn't going to lead them like their God had. Unlike God, a human leader was bound to fall short. Politicians will fail us. Bosses will fail us. Hey, pastors will fail, too! But God never fails us, which is why we are always best served by putting our trust in Him.

Since Israel chose to follow a human king, anyway, they ended up with Saul. Now, Saul looked the part and sounded the part. He came from a family of wealth and influence, and he "was the most handsome man in Israel—head and shoulders taller than anyone else in the land" (1 Samuel 9:1–2). But over time, it became evident that King Saul was an insecure leader who cared what other people thought about him more than he cared what God thought. As a result, he tended to take matters into his own hands instead of trusting God.

Yes, David was also a sinner, and when he eventually became king, he would make more than one misstep. The key difference between these two men was that David trusted in the Lord, even when he missed the mark, while Saul trusted in himself. That's what God noticed about David's heart that qualified him for leadership and ended up disqualifying Saul.

Because Saul wasn't a man after God's own heart, God eventually rejected him as king. Given potential and opportunity, Saul had squandered both, so now David entered the picture. And because in some ways, David was a type, or foreshadowing and reflected image, of Christ, his story began in Bethlehem.

THE PREPARATION OF A KING

Now the LORD said to Samuel, "You have mourned long enough for Saul. I have rejected him as king of Israel, so fill your flask with olive oil and go to Bethlehem. Find a man named Jesse who lives there, for I have selected one of his sons to be my king."

...When they arrived, Samuel took one look at Eliab and thought, "Surely this is the LORD's anointed!"

But the LORD said to Samuel, "Don't judge by his appearance or height, for I have rejected him. The LORD doesn't see things the way you see them. People judge by outward appearance, but the LORD looks at the heart."
—1 Samuel 16:1, 16:6–7

Samuel himself, the spokesman for God—who walked closely with God and carried His prophetic word to the people of Israel—jumped to conclusions and got it wrong. Relying on his natural, human wisdom and biases, Samuel got caught up in the moment and in the outward appearance of Jesse's sons, the potential candidates for king. If you needed more evidence that no man has perfect judgment, especially at first glance, there it is! You won't get it right all the time, any more than Samuel did. (And if you're dating, keep in mind that God looks at the heart first, before a person's appearance.) Thankfully, when it came to identifying the future king of Israel, the Lord corrected Samuel, and the prophet listened.

> But Samuel said to Jesse, "The LORD has not chosen any of these." Then Samuel asked, "Are these all the sons you have?"
>
> "There is still the youngest," Jesse replied. "But he's out in the fields watching the sheep and goats."
> **—1 Samuel 16:10–11**

Jesse had brought out seven of his sons, but he had eight. It seems, as a father, Jesse didn't understand that children have different personalities but are all valuable. To him, maybe, David was just an awkward adolescent always off singing in the hills and fields with his sheep. On top of this, according to Jewish tradition, Jesse may have (incorrectly) thought David was born as a result of adultery and, so, treated him differently from his seven older brothers.[3]

Whatever the reason, Jesse didn't seem to believe in David. Instead, David's father played favorites and didn't bother presenting his youngest son to the prophet until God clued Samuel into Jesse's omission. A father must value every child—no matter his or her age, appearance, personality, parentage, or any other factor—because every child is valuable to God.

Realize that even though we might not always feel visible to other people, maybe not even to our earthly father, this could be because our heavenly Father is hiding us in preparation for a greater purpose. You and I are God's beloved, and He will cause us to shine in front of those who ignore us, discount us, or despise us! They didn't make us, so they can't break us. And they didn't call us, so they can't disqualify us.

> *So Jesse sent for him. He was dark and handsome, with beautiful eyes.*
>
> *And the LORD said, "This is the one; anoint him."*
>
> *So as David stood there among his brothers, Samuel took the flask of olive oil he had brought and anointed David with the oil. And the Spirit of the LORD came powerfully upon David from that day on.*
> **—1 Samuel 16:12–13**

David was "the one"—and so are you, beloved of God! When I planted Discovery Church, some people thought I was too young and that I lacked the necessary education. In other words, they thought I didn't know enough to be a pastor; they assumed I was insufficiently aware of tradition and of how things were supposed to work in a church.

For every anointing and appointing,

there is a process of preparation.

Yet, when I looked at the qualifications for a pastor, I couldn't find "master's degree," nor could I find "pedigree." Instead, I found that God was looking for a man after His own heart! If you're feeling underqualified, or disqualified by others—like I do, too, at times, and like David did sometimes—be assured that having those feelings doesn't make them true. It's what you do with the feelings that matters. In David's case, he told his soul to quiet down and quit being discouraged:

> *Why am I discouraged? Why is my heart so sad? I will put my hope in God! I will praise him again—my Savior and my God!*
> **—Psalm 43:5**

You see, David knew how to deal with his insecurities: he trusted in God. By contrast, Saul didn't know how to deal with his insecurities, and it destroyed him. This is why God revealed to Samuel that David would be the future king of Israel. It's why Samuel anointed David with oil, there in front of the father and brothers who had discounted him, and the Lord God anointed David with the Holy Spirit.

Though David was anointed, he was not yet appointed. For every anointing and appointing, there is a process of preparation, and not every man has the patience for it. As Jesus said, "Many are called, but few are chosen" (Matthew 22:14).

Stop waiting for what you want; instead,

start handling what you have.

So, what was the preparation process to become the king of Israel? It all boiled down to faithfulness.

Faithful in the Field

In preparation for what God had planned, David the boy had to learn to live for the Lord in the present. He couldn't wallow in daydreams about places he'd rather be, things he'd rather be doing, or ways he'd rather be serving. A man after God's heart must be faithful and obedient right where God has placed him!

So it's important we stop insisting that God promote us. Just be faithful in the field to which He has called you! Stop waiting for what you want; instead, start handling what you have. If you haven't heard a new assignment, then focus on being faithful and contented in your current assignment. It's a lesson I had to learn on my road to pastoring a church. When God called me to ministry, I didn't know exactly where I was supposed to be or what position I was supposed to be in, but He taught me to serve wherever the greatest need was.

Right now, God may be directing you to invest yourself somewhere for no apparent reason because you can't see yet that He wants to use the experience to prepare you for something greater. For instance, as a boy, David had learned to take care of sheep that didn't belong to him; they belonged to his dad, Jesse. Was God wasting David's time? Far from it, God was training David to be able to take care of his heavenly Father's sheep—the people of Israel.

Besides, as Jesus put it, "if you are not faithful with other people's things, why should you be trusted with things of your own?" (Luke 16:12). God's plans for us tend to have humble beginnings for a reason.

Faithful in the Familiar

Conventional wisdom tells us that familiarity breeds contempt. In other words, as we become more familiar with someone or something, we tend to become less gracious and considerate; we become too comfortable and lower the standards for our hearts and our behavior. We become less faithful.

We see this in families, especially among people who live in the same household. Maybe now that you've seen what the person you married is like "behind the scenes" on a daily basis, you don't respect her or your relationship like God expects you to. Taking her for granted, you stopped wooing and dating her; you stopped honoring her.

But we also see this loss of faithfulness in people's relationship with God. Take, for example, the proverbial pastor's kids who are raised in the faith and are on fire for God, and who step into serving and leading, but gradually grow desensitized to the awesomeness of God and the wonder of the gospel. Worn down by the labor and routine of it all, they get bored or burnt out. Maybe this is how the prophet Samuel's sons ended up the way they did:

> *As Samuel grew old, he appointed his sons to be judges over Israel. Joel and Abijah, his oldest sons, held court in Beersheba. But they were not like their father, for they were greedy for money. They accepted bribes and perverted justice.*
>
> **—1 Samuel 8:1–3**

After being anointed, David didn't let it go to his head; he didn't immediately get swept up in the world of prophets and politics. Some young men might have begun to despise their humble, familiar life, with such an anointing on their head: "I'm done with you losers and these smelly sheep! See you later!" David, however, went right back to the boring field with his sheep, because God was continuing to prepare him for manhood and leadership.

What looks like humiliation is often part of preparation.

Faithful in the Forgotten

When David's dad forgot about him, it was okay, because the Father to the fatherless was taking care of him. The Lord was David's hope—and He is yours, too! If you feel forgotten, you are mistaken. In preparation for becoming men and leaders after God's heart, we must learn to worship and surrender to our heavenly Father in the seasons of obscurity. What looks like humiliation is often part of our preparation for an acceleration.

In my early days of ministry, little did I know that watching those babies, teaching those toddlers, cleaning the church, and being faithful in honoring my pastors, managers, and leaders were all ways God was preparing me for more. He wanted me to learn to do my job—to obey Him—with excellence and joy, walking in integrity. Little did I know that God was watching my heart and preparing the way for me.

One of the greatest indicators of maturity is

how we handle authority.

What is God using to shape and mold you for the calling in your life? Now is the moment for each of us to declare we will be faithful even when the world seems to have forgotten us.

Faithful in the Future

The ancient Jewish historian Josephus wrote that Samuel whispered in David's ear to inform the boy he was God's chosen future king of Israel.[4] What do you do when God shows you your future but it's still a long way off?

Being faithful in the future means that when we receive information about what lies in front of us, we respond with maturity. One of the greatest indicators of maturity is how we handle authority.

And like we already saw with David the shepherd boy, if we find out we'll be given authority, God expects us not to let it get to our heads. We don't stop what we're already doing because we think we're too good for it; we only move on in our Father's timing. This is because God-approved masculinity knows how to give credit where credit is due: we don't forget that we owe everything good in our past, present, and future to the Lord.

The contrast between Saul and David had much to do with how they handled authority, in terms of their maturity and their heart posture. Despite his moments of failure, David consistently demonstrated humility, while Saul was consistently prideful. We see this difference at work when God, through His prophet Samuel, told King Saul to destroy the Amalekites:

> One day Samuel said to Saul, "It was the LORD who told me to anoint you as king of his people, Israel. Now listen to this message from the LORD! This is what the LORD of Heaven's Armies has declared: I have decided to settle accounts with the nation of Amalek for opposing Israel when they came from Egypt. Now go and completely destroy the entire Amalekite nation—men, women, children, babies, cattle, sheep, goats, camels, and donkeys."
> **—1 Samuel 15:1–3**

In short, God wanted Saul to destroy everything and everyone, and to keep nothing and spare nobody. When Saul made the fateful decision to disobey, it proved to be the last straw for God.

How to Become a Man After God's Own Heart

Saul and his men spared Agag's life and kept the best of the sheep and goats, the cattle, the fat calves, and the lambs— everything, in fact, that appealed to them. They destroyed only what was worthless or of poor quality. Then the LORD said to Samuel, "I am sorry that I ever made Saul king, for he has not been loyal to me and has refused to obey my command."

—1 Samuel 15:9–10

Surely, God would be so impressed with Saul's mercy on Agag, and with his decision not to slaughter God's creatures wastefully, He would let slide a little bending of the rules—a little disobedience—right? Especially if, as Saul claimed when Samuel confronted him afterward, "my troops brought in the best of the sheep, goats, cattle, and plunder to sacrifice to the LORD your God in Gilgal" (1 Samuel 15:20).

Wrong. Saul did what made sense to him and what would please his loot-happy warriors, instead of trusting God's word. To make matters worse, Saul wasn't heartbroken for breaking God's heart with his disobedience. Instead, Saul was only distraught because he'd gotten caught and faced the loss of his authority as a consequence:

Then Saul admitted to Samuel, "Yes, I have sinned. I have

disobeyed your instructions and the LORD's command, for I was afraid of the people and did what they demanded. But now, please forgive my sin and come back with me so that I may worship the LORD."

...And Samuel said to him, "The LORD has torn the kingdom of Israel from you today and has given it to someone else— one who is better than you.
—1 Samuel 15:24–25, 15:28

David, on the other hand, was heartbroken at his own disobedience because he knew his sin grieved God's heart: "For I recognize my rebellion; it haunts me day and night" (Psalm 51:3).

Though our potential may get us opportunities, our heart posture will secure the victory.

God is not looking for perfect men or perfect women. He's looking for hearts fully devoted to Him. Both Saul and David had potential. Though our potential may get us opportunities, our heart posture will secure the victory. The New Testament confirms this truth:

After removing Saul, he made David their king. God testified concerning him: "I have found David son of Jesse, a man after my own heart; he will do everything I want him to do."
—Acts 13:22

Since all men should aspire to be men after God's own heart, we can't help but wonder: how did David become such a man? In what ways did David live his life—before, during, and after his anointing and preparation—to lead God to bestow such a powerful one-line descriptor on a flawed shepherd boy turned king?

How can we, too, become men after God's own heart? Only God can put that kind of heart in us, so we have to seek His presence and surrender ourselves to Him continually.

Seek the Presence of God

You will show me the way of life, granting me the joy of your presence and the pleasures of living with you forever.
—Psalm 16:11

The things of God and the presence of God were terribly neglected during the time of Saul. The ark of God, which symbolized His presence, lay in the hands of the enemy. But when David came to the throne, he took definite steps to reclaim the ark and reestablish Israel's commitment to the presence of the Lord (2 Samuel 6:1–18). Seeking the presence of God was David's priority.

This should be the desire of all of us who want to be men after God's heart! In this world, it's all too easy to end up seeking other things—career success, material possessions, entertainment, human relationships—in place of God's presence in our lives. If we've committed our heart to our Father in heaven, like David did from a young age, we will hunger for His presence to manifest in our life; it will gnaw at our soul when our focus has strayed!

18

When the presence of God is missing in our daily life, we as men will take every possible step to recover it. This might begin with repentance, confession, and forgiveness, and it always requires returning our deepest love, trust, and obedience to Him. In other words, we have to man up, abandon all distractions, and run hard after the presence of the Lord! Like Moses, decide you won't go anywhere without the presence of God (Exodus 33:15).

> *The Word of God will keep us from sin, but sin will keep us from the Word.*

Study the Precepts of God

The Word of God will keep us from sin, but sin will keep us from the Word.[5] The habit of reading the Bible daily will do more than any other thing for the stability, purity, peace, joy, and fruitfulness of the life of a Christian.

> *Men of God must want their life to be shaped and conformed by His word, not by this world.*

The book of Psalms explains the importance and power of Scripture this way:

> *If your law had not been my delight, I would have perished in my affliction.*
> **—Psalm 119:92** *(NIV)*

Is the Word of God our delight? If we aren't feeding on the Word, devouring it in study, do we sense the starvation of our soul? Men of God must want their life to be shaped and conformed by His word, not by this world.

You don't have to wait for a preacher, a podcaster, or a scholar to tell you what the Word of God means. First, you'll need a Bible—I recommend you buy a study Bible if you don't have one. Then, immerse yourself in Scripture. If you don't know where to begin, find a reading plan online or on the Bible App. Learn to feed yourself on the Word, and let the Holy Spirit teach you to "correctly handle the word of truth" (2 Timothy 2:15 NIV).

Sing the Praise of God

> *I will praise the LORD at all times. I will constantly speak his praises.*
> **—Psalm 34:1**

In the Bible, seventy-three psalms are attributed directly to David. Most of the psalms of David were written during his difficult and tough times—yet almost all are either hymns of praise or prayers. It may seem counterintuitive to praise God when the going gets tough, but David understood this fundamental truth of living for the Lord: it's not our power or prominence, how strong or smart we are, that gets us promoted with God, but our praise.

Throughout David's life, we find that truth as a reoccurring thread. At every turn, despite his circumstances, he kept a heart of worship and an attitude of thanksgiving: "I will sing to the LORD all my life; I will sing praise to my God as long as I live" (Psalm 104:33).

Every day, as long as you live, you ought to praise God your Father as an offering and a sign of your trust in Him! Don't just sing to Him on Sunday morning, or only when life seems to be running smoothly, your children are behaving, and your wife is happy. Get comfortable with praising God, and bless His name continually!

Finding and fulfilling the will of God must be the greatest goal of our lives as men.

Serve the Purposes of God

In the New Testament book of Acts, Luke honored David with the ultimate description of a life well-lived:

For David, after he had served the purpose of God in his own generation, fell asleep and was laid with his fathers...
—Acts 13:36 *(ESV)*

One of the important reasons why God called David a man after His own heart is that David was always willing to do God's will and fulfill His desires. Finding and fulfilling the will of God must be the greatest goal of our lives as men. The Bible says, "The eyes of the LORD search the whole earth in order to strengthen those whose hearts are fully committed to him" (2 Chronicles 16:9).

Neither past generations nor future generations can serve God's purpose in *this* generation—only *we* can. God has created us for such a time as this!

Surrender to the Plan of God

When we hear the phrase "surrender to God," we might think that we are going to stop really living. The truth is this: when we surrender, we will finally start living! Surrendering to God means to start living *with a purpose*—the purpose God has planned for us.

Jeremiah 29:11 says, "'For I know the plans I have for you,' declares the LORD, 'plans to prosper you and not to harm you, plans to give you hope and a future.'" God is saying that He has a plan for our lives! We can give up our selfish desires and put our futures in the hands of God, and He will take us far beyond our dreams.

God's ways might be difficult to wrap our minds around fully sometimes, but we're no mystery to Him:

> O LORD, you have examined my heart and know everything about me. You know when I sit down or stand up. You know my thoughts even when I'm far away. You see me when I travel and when I rest at home. You know everything I do. You know everything I am going to say before I say it, LORD.
> **—Psalm 139:1–4**

How does God know us so well? Because He created us!

You made all the delicate, inner parts of my body and knit me together in my mother's womb. Thank you for making me so wonderfully complex! Your workmanship is marvelous—how well I know it.
—Psalm 139:13-14

Not only did God create us, but He also did an amazing job of it. His work is always of the highest quality!

And how, as men, should we respond to this truth? With trust in His ways and His work. When we grow close to God through a meaningful, daily relationship with Him, He helps us to see where we're diverging from His ways or trusting Him incompletely:

Search me, O God, and know my heart; test me and know my anxious thoughts. Point out anything in me that offends you, and lead me along a path of everlasting life.
—Psalm 139:23-24

Ask God to scrape out all of the distrust and disobedience from your soul so His perfect ways and His loving plans for you can shape your life. Let nothing be hidden from God—because the more you man up and surrender to Him, doing what He directs you to do, the more He will help you become a man after His own heart.

Chapter One Questions

Question: What does it mean to you to be a man (or woman) after God's heart?

_____

_____

_____

_____

_____

_____

_____

_____

_____

Question: In what areas of your heart and your life are you being faithful? In what areas of faithfulness do you need to grow?

_____

_____

_____

_____

_____

_____

_____

_____

Question: How well are you focusing on, trusting in, and obeying God in His plans and purpose for you?

_____

_____

_____

_____

_____

_____

_____

_____

_____

_____

_____

_____

Action: Develop a specific plan for nourishing yourself better on the Word of God—daily, weekly, and monthly.

Chapter One Notes

Facing Your Giants

David is probably best known for something he did as a young man, before he became the famed king of Israel: he killed a giant named Goliath.

What many men might not realize is that every one of us faces giants in the course of life, even if they don't typically look like a nine- or ten-foot-tall Philistine warrior.

What giants have shown up in your life?

What giants are you facing right now?

The bigger the destiny God has planned for you, the bigger the giants you will face!

Maybe your current giant looks like a bill you're not sure how to pay. Maybe it's a diagnosis from a doctor. Or maybe your giant takes the form of family dysfunction and discord. For some of us, our giant feels less like Goliath and more like a giant octopus with monstrous tentacles, or perhaps a many-headed hydra from Greek mythology.

Like David, we all face our own giants and we all fall short of God's mark sometimes. But facing a giant doesn't necessarily mean you've made a misstep. In fact, the bigger the destiny God has planned for you, the bigger the giants you will face! From David's story, we can learn a lot about how to take out the inevitable giants in our life.

> *The Philistines now mustered their army for battle and camped between Socoh in Judah and Azekah at Ephesdammim. Saul countered by gathering his Israelite troops near the valley of Elah. So the Philistines and Israelites faced each other on opposite hills, with the valley between them.*
> **—1 Samuel 17:1–3**

A battle occurred between the Israelites and their neighbors because the Philistines were after Israelite territory. Likewise, in each of our lives, territory is at stake: Satan is after our turf! The enemy, Satan, is after the territory of your family, including your marriage and the souls of your children, your future children, and their children through the generations. And of course, Satan wants you—your purity of mind, body, and soul.

God intends our valleys not as moments of defeat but as moments that will define us.

Note that the biblical battle happened in the valley between the opposing armies. Oftentimes, we think the greatest acts of faith must occur on the mountaintops of life, when

God's blessings seem to have propelled us to new heights of earthly success and comfort. In reality, though, we tend to be most reliant on faith when our spiritual enemy attacks us at our low points—in our valleys—and we're all too aware that victory is only possible by the strength of God. When we're feeling discouraged, we ought to take comfort and confidence in the knowledge that God intends our valleys not as moments of defeat but as moments that will define us. Those of us facing a giant today are positioned so God can define us in this moment!

If thinking about our personal giants tempts us to run for the hills in fear—if our faith seems like no match for the enemy we face—keep in mind that Goliath was as intimidating as giants come:

> Then Goliath, a Philistine champion from Gath, came out of the Philistine ranks to face the forces of Israel. He was over nine feet tall! He wore a bronze helmet, and his bronze coat of mail weighed 125 pounds. He also wore bronze leg armor, and he carried a bronze javelin on his shoulder. The shaft of his spear was as heavy and thick as a weaver's beam, tipped with an iron spearhead that weighed 15 pounds.
> **—1 Samuel 17:4–7**

Sure, the giants in our lives might be serious, even deadly serious, but we probably won't have to face a guy who stands more than nine feet tall and wants to put a fifteen-pound spearhead through us. Yet either way, men after God's heart are giant-slayers, like David was. It's easy to imagine David, at the cowboy stage of his life, being eager to test his faith against a literal giant to see if he had what it took to become a warrior in God's service. Goliath's taunts had the older men quaking in their sandals:

> *Goliath stood and shouted a taunt across to the Israelites. "Why are you all coming out to fight?" he called. "I am the Philistine champion, but you are only the servants of Saul. Choose one man to come down here and fight me If he kills me, then we will be your slaves. But if I kill him, you will be our slaves! I defy the armies of Israel today! Send me a man who will fight me!" When Saul and the Israelites heard this, they were terrified and deeply shaken.*
> —*1 Samuel 17:8-11*

But David the "cowboy" shepherd wouldn't be deterred or demoralized by the enemy's verbal attacks. Regardless of what stage you're at, in your journey to recapture the heart of manhood, you can be a giant-killer, too! With this in mind, let's glean some key characteristics from the biblical profile of David, slayer of giants:

BE CONFIDENT IN THE LORD

Sometimes, in ancient and medieval times, two rulers or peoples in conflict would each choose one warrior to serve as their champion. Whichever of the two opposing champions emerged victorious from their duel would decide the victor in the larger conflict, too. In the war between the Israelites and Philistines, Goliath invited the Israelites—with taunts and insults—to fight this kind of representative battle.

We can't get over what God wants to put under us if we refuse to get under whomever God has put over us.

The Philistine giant's physical size and might lent him total confidence in victory, and the Israelites, including King Saul himself, seemed to agree. To defeat Goliath, God's people would need a champion who was also a man of God.

Now David was the son of a man named Jesse, an Ephrathite from Bethlehem in the land of Judah. Jesse was an old man at that time, and he had eight sons. Jesse's three oldest sons—Eliab, Abinadab, and Shimea—had already joined Saul's army to fight the Philistines. David was the youngest son. David's three oldest brothers stayed with Saul's army, but David went back and forth so he could help his father with the sheep in Bethlehem.

For forty days, every morning and evening, the Philistine champion strutted in front of the Israelite army.

One day Jesse said to David, "Take this basket of roasted grain and these ten loaves of bread, and carry them quickly to your brothers. And give these ten cuts of cheese to their captain. See how your brothers are getting along, and bring back a report on how they are doing." David's brothers were with Saul and the Israelite army at the valley of Elah, fighting against the Philistines.

So David left the sheep with another shepherd and set out early the next morning with the gifts, as Jesse had directed him. He arrived at the camp just as the Israelite army was leaving for the battlefield with shouts and battle cries. Soon the Israelite and Philistine forces stood facing each other, army against army. David left his things with the keeper of supplies and hurried out to the ranks to greet his brothers. As he was talking with them, Goliath, the

Philistine champion from Gath, came out from the Philis-
tine ranks. Then David heard him shout his usual taunt to
the army of Israel.

—1 Samuel 17:12–23

Notice here, David was completely honoring and in sub-mission to his father: he helped Jesse with the sheep and also ran errands for him, delivering care packages to his older brothers in Saul's army. We can't get over what God wants to put under us if we refuse to get under whomever God has put over us. In other words, God-approved obedience and sub-mission is a prerequisite for having authority. David showed honor and integrity in his relationship with his father.

Now, when David first heard Goliath shouting challenges at the Israelites, it was already a familiar ritual to the warriors in the two armies; the same thing had been happening for forty days. Of course, hindsight can provide us with a lot of insight, which is why sometimes, when we face one of our giants, we look back and say to ourselves, "Man, I wish I'd done that sooner," or, "You know, I could've handled that better." When we replay events in our minds, we almost always find we could improve on how we handled things. This makes David's response to Goliath's taunts more remarkable: the young shepherd possessed the character and faith to perceive the Israelites' present situation with the clarity and confidence of seeing it in hindsight. If you're wondering why David wasn't impressed or intimidated by Goliath, it wasn't because he was a reckless, cocky, or foolish youth; it was because his faith helped him see clearly!

David asked a few of the Israelite soldiers, "What will a man get for killing this Philistine and ending his defiance of Israel?" (1 Samuel 17:26). From the confident curiosity of David's question, we might imagine he was baffled that the giant had been able to get away with insulting and terrorizing God's people for so long. Through the eyes of faith, a young shepherd could see what others could not: there was no reason someone—some man who truly loved and trusted God—could not have dealt with this situation already.

If you slay the giants in your life, it will change the atmosphere of your home.

If no one else, that "someone" should have been King Saul himself. Saul the Tall, the first man God chose through His prophet Samuel to lead His people, was the person who should have been most qualified to confront the giant. Lacking the necessary faith-filled confidence, Saul acted out of his usual insecurity and decided to delegate his responsibility. The king offered a generous incentive plan to whomever would be man enough for the job:

As soon as the Israelite army saw him, they began to run away in fright. "Have you seen the giant?" the men asked. "He comes out each day to defy Israel. The king has offered a huge reward to anyone who kills him. He will give that man one of his daughters for a wife, and the man's entire family will be exempted from paying taxes!"
—1 Samuel 17:24–25

No taxes for life—for his entire family? Saul wasn't messing around: he wanted someone to step up and save the day so he wouldn't have to. The champion who killed this giant would improve his financial status in a big way; he would also change his social status by marrying the king's daughter. Killing this giant would alter the trajectory of a man's destiny—his whole life!

The way you see God changes how

you approach your giants.

If you slay the giants in your life, it will change the atmosphere of your home. Killing the shame, fear, and worry attached to your secret sin will make a difference in determining whom you marry and where you live. It will transform your relationships and reshape your life. You might be in the shepherd's pasture now, but you could suddenly find yourself in a royal palace. All this can follow from your decision, in faith, to take on your giants—maybe even a single giant. Remember this when Satan taunts you and tries to deceive you into thinking you're unqualified. If you listen to the enemy, you'll never deal with your giants and they will always control you.

David knew better, which is why his response to the standoff between Goliath and the Israelites wasn't just confused; the tone of his words also sounded irritated, even frustrated:

Who is this pagan Philistine anyway, that he is allowed to defy the armies of the living God?
—1 Samuel 17:26

David thought the whole mess was nonsense, as we can tell from the way he slung the Israelite insult "pagan" or "uncircumcised" (NIV) when talking about Goliath. He knew it was wrong for men who claimed to honor God to quiver and run in fear from a giant who dishonored Him and threatened His people. Where fear consumed the Israelite king and soldiers, courage filled David because confidence is a byproduct of how we, as men, see God.

SEE GOD ACCORDING TO WHAT HE SAYS ABOUT HIMSELF

The way you see God changes how you approach your giants. When David fumed, "Who is this pagan Philistine anyway, that he is allowed to defy the armies of the living God?" he made clear, he knew he served a living God. The God of Israel isn't mad, sad, bad, or dead—He is *alive* and searching for giant-killers, the next generation of men who will call on the name of the Lord. Remember what He told Joshua:

No one will be able to stand against you as long as you live. For I will be with you as I was with Moses. I will not fail you or abandon you.
—Joshua 1:5

And knowing that God is faithful, and more powerful than any enemy, giant-killers say with David:

I thirst for God, the living God. When can I go and stand before him?

—Psalm 42:2

Instead of listening to our giants, we need to start listening to what God says, both about Himself and about us!

There are people who know about your history but aren't connected to your destiny.

SEE YOURSELF ACCORDING TO WHAT GOD SAYS ABOUT YOU

But when David's oldest brother, Eliab, heard David talking to the men, he was angry. "What are you doing around here anyway?" he demanded. "What about those few sheep you're supposed to be taking care of? I know about your pride and deceit. You just want to see the battle!"

"What have I done now?" David replied. "I was only asking a question!"

—1 Samuel 17:28–29

As soon as David started raising up a standard against the giant, look who started talking back to him. It wasn't just Goliath; sometimes the insults come from those closest to you. David's brother Eliab accused him of being neglectful, selfish, and dishonest, and treated him as insignificant. Eliab knew about David's history, but he didn't know about David's destiny.

There are people who know about your history but aren't connected to your destiny. Maybe they're insecure about their own circumstances and potential, so they demean you and try to cut down your dreams. They'll try to remind you of who you used to be: what you used to smoke, how much you used to drink, who you used to party with, and what you used to be like.

Thank God for those people who don't remind you of who you used to be, but who see the potential inside of you and believe in who you're called to be! I'm so thankful for the people who saw potential in me. They didn't see me for my past mistakes or current issues. Instead, they saw who I was called to be, and they believed in me.

SEE YOUR CIRCUMSTANCES ACCORDING TO GOD'S WORD

"Don't worry about this Philistine," David told Saul. "I'll go fight him!"

"Don't be ridiculous!" Saul replied. "There's no way you can fight this Philistine and possibly win! You're only a boy, and he's been a man of war since his youth."
—1 Samuel 17:32–33

In God's word, Red Seas can part, Jericho walls can fall down, the blind see, the lame walk, and the sick are healed.

Giants fall! Every time you face a circumstance that the enemy tells you will never change, you need to start seeing it through the lens of God's word. This applies no matter how giant your difficult circumstance looks—how many bills you have to pay, how lonely you feel, or how far away you seem from a healthy marriage and a healthy family.

Your identity is not in your ability.
Your identity is in Christ.

Every giant will fall! God never intended us to live with the giants; He intended us to drive out the giants. It doesn't matter what other people say, what we think, or what our giant says. You are more than a conqueror (Romans 8:37)! You've got what it takes. Your ability to overcome giants doesn't rely on your capabilities. You can do this because God is with you.

KNOW WHO YOU ARE BY KNOWING WHOSE YOU ARE

David knew who he was because he knew whose he was. You are a child of God: God's son, or God's daughter. Your identity is not in your ability. Your identity is not in your stature. It's not in your family, financial status, or past. Your identity is in Christ.

So even if you messed up big-time right before reading this, you are a child of God. He still loves you, is still for you, and still has a plan for you. He will help you take out your giants. Don't let the enemy of self-defeat and condemnation talk you out of God's plan for your life. For many of us today, the giant isn't across the valley; it's in the mirror—in how we see ourselves and in the things we tell ourselves.

Know who you are by knowing whose you are. David knew with every fiber of his being that be belonged to the living God, who would be his helper and protector.

The LORD who rescued me from the claws of the lion and the bear will rescue me from this Philistine!
—1 Samuel 17:37

On the other hand, David knew he could throw stones at Goliath, but he couldn't throw stones at his brother or King Saul. Some of us are in unnecessary battles. We might feel like we have to respond to everybody we cross paths with on social media, but it's not worth it; it's a waste of time and energy.

"What have I done now?" David replied. "I was only asking a question!" He walked over to some others and asked them the same thing and received the same answer.
—1 Samuel 17:29–30

Hey, the dogs bark, but the train keeps rolling. Sometimes people are going to criticize you, falsely accuse you, or make up crazy stories about you, but when you are following God's plan, you just keep moving forward. Don't quit!

And you have to know who the real enemy is. The real enemy is not other people, your spouse, your kids, your in-laws, or your boss. The real enemy is the prince of darkness, who is trying to bring strife and get you distracted fighting unnecessary battles. Don't get hung up on what the Eliabs or the Goliaths in your life are saying. Keep focused on the right fight.

REMEMBER YOUR VICTORIES

We saw David's father Jesse didn't think he had king potential. Saul didn't think he had champion potential. Saul tried to discourage him, but David had been a warrior from his youth. (Remember, men have a bit of the warrior in them at every stage, even boyhood!)

> But David persisted. "I have been taking care of my father's sheep and goats," he said. "When a lion or a bear comes to steal a lamb from the flock, I go after it with a club and rescue the lamb from its mouth. If the animal turns on me, I catch it by the jaw and club it to death. I have done this to both lions and bears, and I'll do it to this pagan Philistine, too, for he has defied the armies of the living God!
> —1 Samuel 17:34–36

What David did back then, he could do again. Keeping sheep might have seemed like a menial, trivial task to David's brother or to King Saul, but David fulfilled that task with honor and courage. Now this Philistine giant was ticking David off, and the "cowboy" shepherd was ready to face Goliath the way he'd faced lions and bears: with the Lord by his side.

We mistakenly remember what we should forget while forgetting what we should remember.

Some of us are just letting the devil beat up on us on a daily basis. Sometimes it's not even what others are saying to us, but what we say to ourselves on the inside: "I'm unworthy. I'm unqualified. I've never fought a giant like this. I don't know how to raise these kids. I don't know how I'm going to get up from this mistake." We beat ourselves up.

And we do this because we mistakenly remember what we should forget while forgetting what we should remember. We tend to hold onto our mistakes, shame, and failures, but God has already forgotten about them. Instead of dwelling on our defeats, He wants us to remember our victories and successes. No matter how difficult things feel in the moment, remind yourself of the facts: you're still breathing, you're still standing, and Satan hasn't won yet. There's time left on the scoreboard, so get up and change toward that giant!

David convinced Saul to let him try, but Saul still lacked confidence:

Saul finally consented. "All right, go ahead," he said. "And may the Lord be with you!"

Then Saul gave David his own armor—a bronze helmet and a coat of mail. David put it on, strapped the sword over it, and took a step or two to see what it was like, for he had never worn such things before.

"I can't go in these," he protested to Saul. "I'm not used to

them." So David took them off again.
—1 Samuel 17:38–39

Saul expected David to struggle in the battle, so he tried to weigh the boy down with heavy armor. But you can't wear the expectations of others as you engage in your assignment. When I sought approval to plant a church, church-planting coaches critiqued a message I preached. It was suggested I was confrontational—that I needed to be more inviting and "dial it down" if I wanted to grow a church. They said I needed to keep it short.

Mediocrity is mass-produced.
Destiny is custom-designed.

I tried—and it wasn't me. I realized I wasn't interested in growing a church the way they meant. My mission was, and is, to reach the lost and make disciples. So I decided I was going to preach with authority and energy, with passion and edge. I was going to preach loud, fast, and long, and act like the clock wasn't there. And for some reason, people came back in greater numbers.

Listen, your anointing flows freely when you tap into the vein of your unique abilities and distinct passions. Mediocrity is mass-produced. Destiny is custom-designed. Don't try to wear someone else's armor into battle.

*Stop talking **about** your giant, and start talking **to** your giant.*

SPEAK FAITH TO YOUR GIANT

The devil wants to scare you and silence you. Don't let the giants do all the talking. You need to control the volume in the valley. You need to control the narrative. You can't overcome the giant in your life by staying silent, because your words matter; they hold power.

Let me say it this way: stop talking *about* your giant, and start talking *to* your giant. Don't waste your time complaining to everyone around you about your situation. I've learned that if you don't talk to your giants, your giants will talk to you instead—and giants can say some nasty, unhelpful things.

He picked up five smooth stones from a stream and put them into his shepherd's bag. Then, armed only with his shepherd's staff and sling, he started across the valley to fight the Philistine.

Goliath walked out toward David with his shield bearer ahead of him, sneering in contempt at this ruddy-faced boy. "Am I a dog," he roared at David, "that you come at me with a stick?" And he cursed David by the names of his gods. "Come over here, and I'll give your flesh to the birds and wild animals!" Goliath yelled.

—1 Samuel 17:40–44

You may speak to your giant and find your situation looks the same, month after month, in the natural realm. Don't worry about it. In the unseen realm, things are changing in your favor!

Jesus spoke to bad weather, water, fevers, sickness, dead people and demons, and they all obeyed Him when He spoke. And He tells us, too, to speak to our problems in His name:

> *I tell you the truth, anyone who believes in me will do the same works I have done, and even greater works, because I am going to be with the Father. You can ask for anything in my name, and I will do it, so that the Son can bring glory to the Father. Yes, ask me for anything in my name, and I will do it!*
>
> **—John 14:12–14**

One time, Jesus spoke to a fig tree (Mark 11:12–14) that didn't have any fruit ready for Him to eat. He decided to use it as an opportunity to teach His disciples something, so He cursed the tree. Jesus didn't pray about the fig tree. He didn't say, "I'm believing it's not going to produce any fruit." No, He commanded it not to produce fruit.

But Jesus walked away, and it didn't look like anything had happened. The tree appeared outwardly just as healthy and green as it was before. I'm sure some of His disciples whispered, "It didn't work. Jesus must be losing His touch."

The reality is, the moment He spoke, that tree started dying. The next morning, when night was over, they saw the fig tree dead. We go through a time of darkness when it will look like nothing is happening, but don't be fooled: daybreak is coming, and then you will see results!

A breakthrough for me was realizing that my giants

respond to my voice. That's why they try to silence you by drowning you out with noise and fear. Notice that David didn't get sucked into an insult contest with Goliath:

> David replied to the Philistine, "You come to me with sword, spear, and javelin, but I come to you in the name of the LORD of Heaven's Armies—the God of the armies of Israel, whom you have defied. Today the LORD will conquer you, and I will kill you and cut off your head. And then I will give the dead bodies of your men to the birds and wild animals, and the whole world will know that there is a God in Israel!
>
> **—1 Samuel 17:45–46**

David called things according to his knowledge of the truth and his trust in God. "In the name of the LORD"—by His power. "Today the LORD *will*"—there was no doubt. The battle belonged to the Lord.

Don't hide. Don't run to the caves. Don't get silent. You show up and speak faith to your giant!

Don't dwell on it. Deal with it!

ATTACK YOUR GIANT QUICKLY

The longer you wait, the bigger the giant gets. The longer you let an addiction build in your house, the bigger it gets. The day that David heard the giant talking was the same day that David took the giant out.

As Goliath moved closer to attack, David quickly ran out to meet him.

—1 Samuel 17:48

He didn't wait two weeks or ten years. He didn't say, "Let me play the field a little bit." *No!* Don't dwell on it—deal with it!

What giant are you facing today? What giant has been taking control of territory in your life? Deal with it! Say, "I've got an appointment with my destiny right here. There is an award on the other side of my obedience." Attack the giant quickly!

You would think the closer you get to the giant in your life, the bigger it becomes. The opposite is actually true. The closer we get to our fear, and to the lies of the enemy keeping us back, the more clearly we can see through the illusion that has been limiting our life.

Reaching into his shepherd's bag and taking out a stone, he hurled it with his sling and hit the Philistine in the forehead. The stone sank in, and Goliath stumbled and fell face down on the ground.

So David triumphed over the Philistine with only a sling and a stone, for he had no sword.

—1 Samuel 17:49–50

Despite what Saul and the rest of the warriors expected, it didn't take a sword or a spear to defeat Goliath. It took a simple sling and a stone.

What we might instinctively think we need to overcome

the giant is not what we really need. We don't need the weapons of this world. We don't fight like this world, because our weapons are heavenly. Our weapons are mighty for pulling down strongholds (2 Corinthians 10:4)! There's always a vulnerable spot in the enemy's plan, and the Lord will show you what it is. He will give you the strategy to take the giant out.

CUT THE HEAD OFF THE GIANT

David also teaches us something about how to finish killing our giant. He went over to the giant, stood over Goliath like a boss, and used his fallen enemy's own sword to decapitate his body:

> Then David ran over and pulled Goliath's sword from its sheath. David used it to kill him and cut off his head.
> —*1 Samuel 17:51*

There's a finality to cutting off the head of your enemy: Take divorce off the table. Change your phone. Block the caller. Change your job. Move to another state if you have to. Set up a healthy boundary. Cut the head off!

Greater is He who is in you (that is, God) than he who is in the world (that is, Satan) (1 John 4:4). Deal decisively with the enemy of your soul, confident in the Lord who reigns in your soul!

BE A GIANT-KILLER

If we want to be giant-killers after God's own heart, we need to see clearly, act confidently, and walk humbly, as David did. You might find yourself in a valley today. You might be facing a giant right now. But no matter how fearsome the giant seems, or how many giants there are, the battle is the Lord's, which means victory is assured if you rely on Him.

Then, when God defeats your giant in the valley for you and gives you a mountain, stay humble as the enemy tries to attack you through your pride and ego. Remember who gave you the victory and put you on that mountain in the first place: it wasn't you.

Like David was God's champion fighting on behalf of Israel, Jesus stepped out onto the spiritual battlefield on our behalf: "And having disarmed the powers and authorities, he made a public spectacle of them, triumphing over them by the cross" (Colossians 2:15 NIV). Christ has disarmed and triumphed over the enemy on the cross, cutting the head off of Satan's plan to kill, steal, and destroy what God has planned for you. The victory is already yours, so stop responding to your fear and the expectations of the world. Respond to your faith by putting on the armor of Christ today, and your giant won't stand a chance.

Chapter Two Questions

Question: What's the biggest giant you're facing in your life currently? What lies are you hearing from your giant, or from other people, about you or your circumstances?

_____

_____

_____

_____

_____

_____

_____

_____

Question: What truths about God, your circumstances, and your identity can you use to counter the lies you're hearing?

_____

_____

_____

_____

_____

_____

_____

Question: What is the most important truth or promise of God that you need to speak to your giant today? How exactly will you do this?

_____

_____

_____

_____

_____

_____

_____

_____

_____

_____

_____

_____

Action: Develop a plan of battle against your giant. What spiritual equipment do you need? What overall strategy and specific tactics will you use? What will it look like to attack your giant quickly and "cut off its head"?

Chapter Two Notes

CHAPTER THREE

Waiting in the Wilderness

God's heart was broken. Israel didn't want God as king; they wanted a human king like all the other nations. God chose Saul, who was a good candidate, but he was more self-interested than God-interested. This showed up in a lot of ways, so God removed His Spirit from Saul. Then God identified a new leader for His people: David, a young shepherd from the house of Jesse. God chose David because he was a man after God's own heart.

When Saul and the armies of Israel lacked the faith and courage to defeat their enemies, David manned up and killed the giant named Goliath. With his stones and sling, David took out the Philistine champion defying the armies of the living God. This catapulted David into instant fame, as he became a living legend.

All of a sudden, David was a household name. People were cheering him in the streets. Girls were talking about him. *Everybody* was talking about David! If he'd had a line of sneakers, everybody would've been wearing them. If Instagram were around, he would've been an instafamous internet sensation. But this apparent high point was the beginning of a long season of troubles for David.

DODGING SPEARS

Saul's decision to have David stick by his side instead of returning home to his family might not seem like much, but that was the beginning of the control Saul was bringing down on David. There was a spirit of control in Saul—a manipulative, dominating spirit. It was a manipulative spirit that didn't want David to stay connected with his own family:

> *From that day Saul kept David with him and did not let him return home to his family.*
> **—1 Samuel 18:2** *(NIV)*

Saul didn't even want his son Jonathan to be David's friend, so he tried to drive a wedge between them. Saul wanted David's only relationship to be with Saul; he wanted his own voice to be the only one speaking into David's life. This was what we'd call a toxic situation.

We might believe we have a Saul in our life—that boss or other person who gets on our nerves. But we shouldn't assign the "Saul" label lightly. It's not the person who's demanding you get to work on time—you need to do that. Someone isn't a Saul for demanding you do your job. It's not the person who's confronting you on problem areas in which you need to grow. Those things are just part of being a good boss or a good friend. And a father isn't a Saul for expecting his children's obedience or for teaching them to forgive, get along, and love each other.

In stark contrast, the biblical Saul was a madman doing everything he could to kill David and destroy his purpose. A Saul is someone who trolls you, gossips about you, makes up rumors about you, slanders you, and cheers when you fall or falter. Sauls pray that you fail, and they do everything they can to make your life miserable.

Comparison always clouds the clarity of your calling.

Every one of us should pause right now, look inward, and ask the Holy Spirit to point out if there's a Saul in our own heart. Are you harboring jealousy, paranoia, suspicion, or insecurity? Do you want to get even with someone who has hurt or offended you, or undermine someone who threatens you somehow? It's easier than you might think, dangerously easy, for an evil spirit to take up residence in your heart the way it did in Saul's.

Whatever mission Saul sent him on, David was so successful that Saul gave him a high rank in the army. This pleased all the troops, and Saul's officers as well. When the men were returning home after David had killed the Philistine, the women came out from all the towns of Israel to meet King Saul with singing and dancing, with joyful songs and with timbrels and lyres. As they danced, they sang: "Saul has slain his thousands, and David his tens of thousands."
—1 Samuel 18:5–7

I don't care who you are: that scenario would make any of us, in Saul's shoes, stop and say, "Wait a minute. Why do you have to say it like that? Why do you have to make a comparison between us?" The world will compare you: "You're not like your brother or your sister." "I wish you could act more like them." "I wish you could do that." The world will draw you into comparison, but you don't have to buy into it; you don't have to let that spirit of comparison get inside you.

> *Saul was very angry; this refrain displeased him greatly. ...*
> *And from that time on Saul kept a close eye on David.*
> **—1 Samuel 18:8–9**

Because Saul's eyes were not on God, they drifted to fixate on David. Comparison always clouds the clarity of your calling. As long as you're comparing yourself to someone else, you can't see clearly the race the Lord has called you to run. When you're running a race and your eyes shift away from God, toward other people, you'll miss your turns.

There's nobody like you in the world! The more you see who you are in Christ, the more you can celebrate with those who are succeeding beside you.

Saul's eyes deviated from his own race and started to dwell on David running his race. Comparison leads to envy, jealousy, and destruction. Don't let it destroy your life like it did to Saul! If you're on the road to comparison, stop—before you find yourself trying to turn other people into pincushions:

The next day an evil spirit from God came forcefully on Saul. He was prophesying in his house, while David was playing the lyre, as he usually did. Saul had a spear in his hand and he hurled it, saying to himself, "I'll pin David to the wall." But David eluded him twice. Saul was afraid of David, because the LORD was with David but had departed from Saul.

—1 Samuel 18:10–12 *(NIV)*

Whoa! David was probably just innocently singing, "As the deer longs for streams of water, so I long for you, O God" (Psalm 42:1), and there was Saul, glaring at him and sharpening his spear. What's worse, David was only there singing because Saul wanted him there to calm him down. Saul, who had shown such potential, had become broken by the weight of trying to be a leader in his own strength, forsaking the anointing of God. For David's troubles, Saul tried to pin him to the wall with a deadly weapon, and it wasn't the only time this happened.

Now, if you're David, what do you do when someone throws a spear at you? Not actual spears, for most of us, but verbal spears, like accusations from other people or lies from the enemy. We can get angry and try to get revenge, picking up a spear of our own and throwing it back. We can become afraid and respond by becoming discouraged and defensive. How we respond to attacks reveal the depth of our maturity.

THE SACRED SCHOOL OF BROKENNESS

Most people think David stepped right into the kingdom after defeating Goliath, but that misconception skips over fifteen years of his life. He had to become the king of the caves before he could become the king of Israel! The feat of slaying Goliath that was supposed to launch him into leadership actually dropped him into the deepest, darkest, most difficult valley he had ever walked through.

Brokenness always precedes breakthrough.

In other words, David enrolled in the School of Brokenness. You see, God has a university. Very few enroll in it, and even fewer graduate. It is a school for men, and women, who desire to be more like Jesus. And in that desire, God uses the adversities that come against them to break them—so that He can use them to bring healing to a broken world.

David was enrolling into God's sacred School of Brokenness and didn't even know it. He was about to walk through his darkest valley, his most difficult years, but this season would prepare him to be king. God would use King Saul's madness to break David's heart so that David would never become like Saul. Brokenness always precedes breakthrough.

We're usually walking through life looking for the easy way, looking to Jesus for a kind of Christian pick-me-up. I have to break it to you: Jesus never promised us a perfect life. He did promise to be a perfect Savior through every season of life. He didn't promise there wouldn't be storms in life, but He did promise to be your shelter in the storm, your refuge, and your stronghold.

When you deny your humanity, you reject all humility.

The reality is, you won't be following Jesus for long if you can't handle the pain. There is no crown without the cross. God's not looking for men who pretend to have it all together and think, "I'm good." To the contrary, He's looking for the broken men who at times will say, with David:

> *I am exhausted from crying for help; my throat is parched. My eyes are swollen with weeping, waiting for my God to help me.*
>
> **—Psalm 69:3**

When you deny your humanity, you reject all humility. So, what do you do when you're in the season of waiting in the wilderness? Acknowledge the reality that times of waiting and moments of difficulty are hard. But don't dwell on that point, either; don't pity yourself. Instead, stay focused on God and His promises.

Otherwise, delays can cause you to drift from your purpose. Enthusiasm and passion slowly dim the longer we're in the waiting rooms of life. We're tempted to retreat, regroup, and recover, like I want to do after a trip to the doctor or the DMV. But delays are not denials. God's "not yet" is *not* a "not ever." God sees what you can't see, so His timing is perfect.

Knowing this, what are the best ways to respond when we find ourselves stuck in the wilderness? Let's face it: a lot of our life will be spent waiting, so we'd better get a handle on this. What do we do when we expected to become king but we find ourselves retreating to a cave?

DON'T STAY ISOLATED

It's tempting to turn your wilderness into a cave of isolation. Yet, if we're willing to surrender our heart to the Lord, the cave of isolation can become a cave of reconciliation and redemption.

> *So David left Gath and escaped to the cave of Adullam.*
> *Soon his brothers all his other relatives joined him there.*
> *—1 Samuel 22:1*

In his cave, David found the opportunity to reconnect with his family—with his brothers and his father, who previously had seemed to brush him off and demean him. Do you need reconciliation in your family or in your other relationships? If you sow loyalty in the waiting, you'll reap loyalty. If you sow honor in the waiting, you'll reap honor. If you sow kindness in the waiting, you'll reap kindness. David had always honored Jesse, and now he reaped honor in return, as his family came to join him in a desperate moment.

> *Then others began coming—men who were in trouble or*
> *in debt or who were just discontented—until David was*
> *the captain of about 400 men.*
> *—1 Samuel 22:2*

All those who were in distress or in debt or discontented also gathered around him, and he became their commander.

About four hundred men were with him, in all. They came to the cave in distress, but they left as men of valor and renown. When you leave this cave, you might have come in weak, but you're coming out strong. You might have come in poor, but you're going out rich. You might have come in stressed, but you're going out with peace. You might enter the cave overwhelmed and defeated, but you're walking out victorious!

The Lord developed David's character in the cave so he could withstand the pressures of the crown.

DON'T GIVE UP

Abraham waited for a son. Jacob waited for Rachel. Don't be surprised if God is using tough times in your life to test your faithfulness.

As difficult as it is to understand, He can use your pain for His purpose. We like to wonder: Why do bad things happen to good people? Why do we have to suffer? Why is life so difficult sometimes? These questions prompt many people to drop out prematurely from the School of Brokenness. Well, no matter where suffering and difficulties originate, God uses tough times to prepare you for something. The Lord developed David's character in the cave so he could withstand the pressures of the crown.

Trusting there is a purpose, faithful people keep on keeping on when other people choose to give up. Faithful people are diligent and determined. They man up. They are persistent. They change their perspective and focus on God's promises in His word. Here's the reality: God is more interested in who you are becoming than what you are accomplishing. He is producing something in you while you wait with courage and integrity.

Also, remember that although you're waiting for something, you already have Someone. Whatever you are waiting for is not more important than God and your relationship with Him. Waiting is part of the School of Brokenness.

> *David now stayed in the strongholds of the wilderness and in the hill country of Ziph. Saul hunted him day after day,* ***but God*** *didn't let Saul find him.*
> —***1 Samuel 23:14*** *(emphasis added)*

Faithful people also understand the concept of "but God": our circumstances or the apparent odds of our survival and success may seem dismal, *but God* is continually at work. God is measuring your heart and molding it to fit your destiny. And don't give up before your biggest "but God" moment—when God moves powerfully and visibly to transform your circumstances in ways you never could have accomplished on your own.

DON'T THROW SPEARS

Saul tried to kill David twenty-one times, but man cannot stop what God has ordained. "No weapon formed against you shall prosper" (Isaiah 54:17 NKJV).

An offended heart is a breeding ground for deception.

So don't get caught throwing spears back at those who offend or persecute you. It's tempting, I know! You don't want to be seen as a doormat. The culture of the world and of social media encourages us to counterattack against those who pick fights with us. Maybe it seems like a good idea to launch a preemptive strike, throwing the first spear to get in the first word and establish our narrative before our opponents can shut us down. That's what it means to man up in today's world, right?

Don't restore relationship with manipulative people
without seeing the fruit of repentance and humility.

Wrong. An offended heart is a breeding ground for deception. Satan wants you to get offended so he can put lies in your heart, like when he filled Saul's heart with suspicion and jealousy toward David.

Can you imagine how offended David must have felt after all those times he fought Saul's battles, defeated the king's enemies, and played music for him to soothe his spirit? Yet, when the opportunity came for revenge, David passed:

So David and Abishai went to the army by night, and there
was Saul, lying asleep inside the camp with his spear stuck
in the ground near his head. Abner and the soldiers were
lying around him. Abishai said to David, "Today God has
delivered your enemy into your hands. Now let me pin him

to the ground with one thrust of the spear; I won't strike
him twice." But David said to Abishai, "Don't destroy him!
Who can lay a hand on the LORD's anointed and be guilt-
less?

—*1 Samuel 26:7–9 (NIV)*

It would have been so easy for David to solve his problems "with one thrust of the spear"; it seemed perfectly logical and justified to do so. David just took Saul's spear and water jug and slipped away. When Saul woke up and realized what had happened, he said:

I have sinned. Come back, David my son. Because you con-
sidered my life precious today, I will not try to harm you
again. Surely I have acted like a fool and have been terribly
wrong.

—*1 Samuel 26:21*

Now, David was too wise to believe Saul's deceitful words of repentance. Don't restore relationship with manipulative people without seeing the fruit of repentance and humility. In his wisdom, David was demonstrating far more maturity than Saul, even though the king was much older than him.

Remember, one of the greatest indicators of maturity is how we handle authority. Saul handled it poorly, becoming insecure and treating people unjustly. Another of the greatest indicators of maturity is how we submit to authority. The kingdom of heaven isn't a democracy; it's a theocracy, with God as our perfect King. He doesn't need to submit His decisions to us, the citizens of His kingdom, for approval. In

God's kingdom, we have to learn to submit to Him and to serve Him, and He also expects us to submit to certain people—for instance, to our father and mother (Exodus 20:12).

Everyone can act like a servant. The true test is: can you still be a servant after you've been treated like one? Can you be a faithful servant when God expects you to wait in obedience? David proved he could, and so can you, if you trust in the authority of God and rely on Him for justice.

DON'T STAY SILENT

It's a common misconception that waiting patiently for God's timing means being passive, sitting on our hands or twiddling our thumbs. Worship while you wait! David knew praising God through song both honors God and helps us withstand our waiting in the wilderness.

It's the praising life that honors me. As soon as you set your foot on the Way, I'll show you my salvation.
—Psalm 50:23 *(MSG)*

And if you read through David's psalms, you'll find they are genuine expressions of God-style praise and worship, which sometimes don't look at all like Sunday-morning praise and worship in churches across our nation. In fact, the psalms of David look more like Friday night at the football game. There's clapping, shouting, dancing, and instruments—all-around exuberant noise!

Most of us grew up in a sports-oriented culture. And when you get enthusiastic at the game, traveling to away games and tailgating and cheering in the stands, people might look at you and say, "Man that's a real fan!" Yet, if you do the same thing on Sunday in church, they call you a real fanatic, instead: "What's that all about?" You're considered weird.

I want to give you seven Hebrew words for *praise* to help you better understand what it means to worship like a man after God's own heart.

Self-conscious, low-key, conservative praise does nothing but protect and conserve our egos.

Halel

Halel shows up simply as "praise" in English-language Bibles. It means "to rave, boast, celebrate"; it means to be "clamorously foolish."[6] You probably recognize this one because this is where we get the expression *hallelujah*. The *-jah* part means "God." So *hallelujah* means to *halel* God. Like David, we ought to act like raving fools in our praise of the Lord—because God likes when we celebrate Him to the point of getting a little bit crazy! He likes to show up and be greeted with excitement at His presence. It makes perfect sense.

While most of us are conditioned to think such unreserved enthusiasm makes total sense at a football game, too many men are conditioned to think it's irreverent behavior for a Sunday morning. It's not, because God is looking for men who are excited to see Him!

David, being pursued by Saul, declared to God:

> *I will thank you in front of the great assembly. I will praise [halel, being clamorously foolish] you before all the people.*
> —**Psalm 35:18**

In other words, to *halel* means to express, "God, I'm just going to celebrate You with all that I am!" By contrast, I believe that self-conscious, low-key, conservative praise does nothing but protect and conserve our egos. We should never be ashamed to give God the praise He wants and deserves—which is your passionate worship.

Now look, if you're resistant to that idea, I'm sympathetic, because I didn't get it, either. I was more conservative in worship when I was younger in my faith. But David's example challenges us to take a step toward less-restrained worship of our God.

Yada

With this second Hebrew word, *yada*, we also just find the English word *praise* in our Bibles. Literally, it means "with the extended hand." But figuratively, it means "to acknowledge in public."[7]

I will praise [yada, acknowledging] you, LORD, with all my heart.

—Psalm 138:1 (NIV)

We can think of it as acknowledging God with an extended hand. For example, if I asked a congregation on Sunday morning, "How many of you in this room are Christians?" most wouldn't even hesitate; they would say, "That's me!" and lift their hand to acknowledge they follow Christ. God likes it when you lift your hands and acknowledge him in worship. After all, who doesn't like to be acknowledged in public? So the lifting of our hands in praise and worship has a purpose.

I love seeing the growth and development of people's worship: to see people who have been hesitant to engage God with their praise begin to express their love and joy freely is so amazing! It's not just an emotional thing; it's more about honor, love, and gratitude toward an awesome God.

Barak

When we think of people presenting themselves before a king, we often imagine them kneeling, or at the very least bowing, out of respect. Well, God is our Father, but He is also our King—and *barak* literally means to bless by kneeling or bowing.[8] It conveys an image of presenting yourself to someone and submitting in reverence to that person. If you want a single-word translation, I suggest the word *surrender*. When you come to God and *barak* before Him, you're saying, "I belong to You now."

Isn't it interesting that the word *praise* could mean something as exuberant and undignified as *halal*, or it could mean something as sober and peaceful as *barak*?

> *Let all that I am [my soul, my emotions] praise [barak, surrendering and submitting to] the* LORD; *with my whole heart, I will praise his holy name.*
> **—Psalm 103:1**

David went on to say, in this psalm, that when we praise God in surrender, He will provide for us: forgiving us, redeeming us, and giving us love, mercy, righteousness, and justice. "He fills my life with good things" (Psalm 103:5), David sang.

Barak, then, is a beautiful expression of worship—just to come to God and say, "Here I am, I surrender to You."

Zamar

The formal definition of the Hebrew word *zamar*, for *praise*, is about making music to God with stringed instruments.[9] The word doesn't convey the sense of some stringed instrument you'd hear while getting a spa treatment, though. The meaning of *zamar* is more like, "Praise God with the stringed instruments, and pluck those bad boys hard!" The word *zamar* tells us He likes it when you get the electric going! (See, God doesn't have to try to be cool—He *is* cool.)

It is good to praise [zamar, hitting those strings and jamming on that guitar] the LORD and make music to your name, O Most High.

—Psalm 92:1 *(NIV)*

Put *zamar* together with *halel* and you have some serious worship going on. In fact, you get Psalm 150, the last chapter in the book of Psalms—where "praise" is a translation of *halel*:

Praise him with a blast of the ram's horn ["sounding of the trumpet" in the NIV]; praise him with the lyre and harp! Praise him with the tambourine and dancing; praise him with the strings and flute! Praise him with a clash of cymbals; praise him with loud clanging cymbals.

—Psalm 150:3–5

Let this psalm be an encouragement to those of us who see this kind of praise in God's word but don't think we're ready to go there yet. Men who love the Lord need to stop fighting it!

Reading through the book of Psalms, I find myself thinking it's crazy how strict many churches' stances against dancing are. I once heard someone say their church is against premarital sex because it might lead to dancing. I don't care what you say—that's funny. But if that description contains a grain of truth about your opinions about "proper Christian behavior," you probably ought to see David and the Psalms for an attitude adjustment.

And notice how Psalm 150 emphasizes the cymbals—in

all their glorious noisiness! Sometimes Christians complain, "It's just too loud in my church." If it's too loud for you in Sunday morning worship, you're not going to like heaven. Better bring your earplugs! You're not even going to be able to hear yourself with all the praise coming up before our God. And God likes that.

Wouldn't you hate it if you were at a football game and someone was like, "Shhh.... All ninety thousand of you, *shhh! I'm trying to watch the game." Who does that? What a joke! The louder the better, right? This is God's way of worship.

Shabach

Yet another biblical word for *praise* is *shabach*, meaning "to address in a loud tone, to shout."[10] (To pronounce this word, you'd better clear the back of your throat and make sure you're not standing too close to anyone!) Yes, the fact of the matter is that in the in the book of Psalms—scriptures that are three thousand years old—we find the people of God praising Him with loud voices and shouts.

This is why, years ago, I made up my mind that I would not scream and shout for a sports team that doesn't know me yet keep silent for the God who made me! David put it this way in one of his songs to the Lord:

> *Your unfailing love is better than life itself [including golf, football, shopping, our kids, blue skies, lake houses, the beach, and all the rest!); how I praise [shabach, shouting to] you! I will praise [shabach, loudly worshiping] you as long as I live, lifting up my hands to you in prayer.*
> *—Psalm 63:3-4*

In short, David said, "God, I'm going to worship You with all I've got." And every man with a heart committed fully to the Lord will man up and do the same.

Towdah

It's no coincidence that of two of these seven words for praise refer to lifting our hands. *Towdah* means "to lift hands in adoration."[11] God likes when we raise our hands in worship! But this one is a little different from the first. If *yada* is like, "Oh, oh, oh, I'm a Christian! I acknowledge You," this one is hands lifted in adoration—and really, in surrender.

So it would be like saying, "Okay, Lord, I give up." It's where you come to God and say, "I give You my life today. And I'm surrendering all that I am to You today. So I let go of all of my pride, my life, my stuff." That's why sometimes when I pray with people in my church, I'll say, "Open your hands." I'm trying to point them toward this idea and act of *towdah*.

He who offers praise [towdah, open-handed surrender] glorifies Me; and to him that orders his conversation aright I will show the salvation of God.
—Psalm 50:23 (NKJV)

I encourage you to stop hanging on to your life, start realizing that you're not that good at being the lord of your own life, and let the Lord your God take control of your life. Let it go. Isn't that surrender beautiful?

Worship is love expressed.

Tehilah

The last of these seven words is, I think, the funniest. Because the seventh word is *tehilah*—"exuberant singing"[12]—which sounds to me like "tequila." But it's not that!

> *I will extol ["praise" in NLT] the LORD at all times; his [tehilah] will always be on my lips*
> **—Psalm 34:1 (NIV)**

Some of us might mishear that translation read out loud and think, "I found my verse," but hold on! Tequila might also produce loud, enthusiastic singing, but it's not the same thing.

Yet, God does enjoy exuberant singing, which means singing you're engaged in emotionally. Don't stay silent, because worship is love expressed. So it's not worship if it's not love, and it's not worship if it's not expressed. We can't say we only love someone in our heart—"Well, I just love God in my heart." I can't tell my wife, "I love you, but don't expect any hugs. I'm not going to touch you. In fact, I don't even like to say it out loud; you just need to know I love you." She wouldn't be too happy about that attitude. Why would God be okay with it? Let's man up and worship God the way He likes to be worshiped.

You will be most tempted to quit when you are the closest to your calling.

DON'T WASTE YOUR WILDERNESS

Make your wilderness a training ground. You will be most tempted to quit when you are the closest to your calling. While some of our wildernesses are caused by our own foolishness and disobedience, many wilderness experiences are designed by God for our good.

Wildernesses come in the form of:

- A disruption to our comfort zone.

- A delay of our timetable.

- A death of our dream.

- A challenge to our character.

- A season of heat, pain, dryness, disappointment, or pressure in our lives.

We all go through things like these. What we do in and with our wilderness experiences is critical to our future. We can waste them, or we benefit from them like David did.

David was greatly distressed because the men were talking of stoning him; each one was bitter in spirit because of his sons and daughters [being captured]. But David found strength in the LORD his God.

—1 Samuel 30:6 *(NIV)*

No one can worship for you. Even the prayers spoken over you cannot sustain your wilderness; you need to lift *your* voice. It's an expression of trust in the Lord that He will be your strength and carry you through, as He did for David when his enemies, the Amalekites, had captured his and his men's families and created discontent among his army.

David fought them from dusk until the evening of the next day, and none of them got away, except four hundred young men who rode off on camels and fled. David recovered everything the Amalekites had taken, including his two wives. Nothing was missing: young or old, boy or girl, plunder or anything else they had taken. David brought everything back.

—1 Samuel 30:17–19 *(NIV)*

Some distance away, in Israel, another battle was taking place, in which the Philistines were defeating Saul and his son, Jonathan (1 Samuel 31). By the end of that battle, Saul and Jonathan would be dead, paving the way for David to become king; yet, in the very moment that was playing out, David remained unaware. Maybe you're on the verge of giving up today because you feel defeated and plundered, while on a different field, God is making a way to victory for you. He will bring everything back to you that belongs to you, and more.

So be encouraged in the Lord! Encourage yourself in the Word of God. There is purpose in the waiting and in your pain.

Even when it hurts and its confusing, say, "God, I don't understand, but I speak words of faith to my mind that cannot comprehend the mysteries of your Spirit. I speak words to my soul and my emotions. What do You want me to learn in this season of waiting? How can I make the most of my time in this wilderness?"

And put your trust in Him.

Chapter Three Questions

Question: What is an example of a "wilderness" season or situation in your life, past or present? What has trusting God during your wilderness waiting required of you?

_____

_____

_____

_____

_____

_____

_____

_____

Question: What "Sauls" have you encountered in your life? How have you responded to them? What would it look like to respond more like a man after God's heart?

_____

_____

_____

_____

_____

_____

_____

Question: Which biblical terms for "praise" explained in this chapter seem most comfortable to you in your own expressions of worship? Which terms of praise sound least comfortable to you? Why do you think these forms of praise are uncomfortable for you?

_____

_____

_____

_____

_____

_____

_____

_____

_____

_____

_____

Action: Choose a term or style of praise discussed in this chapter that falls outside your comfort zone. Each day this week, take time to deliberately worship God in that way!

Chapter Three Notes

_____

_____

_____

_____

_____

_____

_____

_____

_____

_____

_____

_____

_____

_____

_____

_____

_____

Serving Like a King, Leading Like a Shepherd

If Samuel had anointed you, what would you be tempted to do? How would you be tempted to act if the crowds sang your praises in the streets (or on social media)? If you're eager to reach the king stage of masculinity—to be a leader of men, like David the warrior became—your path begins with the humility of David the shepherd boy.

Humility means you have a lowly view of self, an exalted view of God, and a submission to God's will. It's a sober view of oneself, realizing we are nothing without the Lord. David was humble; after all, he had spent the formative years of his life around smelly sheep, yet he consistently trusted and obeyed God and the authority of his father during those years. As his authority grew, he led with the humility of a shepherd: he wasn't spoiled by honor, and he freely confessed his weaknesses. He gave God the glory for what he accomplished, continually pointing people back toward Him.

David knew that "self-made" men don't achieve very much. God was with him, and he also had a team of other people who supported him. Because of David's faithful, humble heart, God gave him the respect of, and leadership over, other mighty warriors. As men, we all need a brotherhood, a group of faithful men to do battle alongside.

Stop using your circumstances as an

excuse to be mediocre.

MIGHTY MEN

The Bible refers to David's mighty men—his "mightiest warriors" (2 Samuel 23:8), including "the Three (who were among the Thirty—an elite group among David's fighting men)" (2 Samuel 23:13). We can guess that these captains were Israelite men at the peak of the warrior stage of manhood, which is why Samuel 23 lists them by name, along with the greatest feats and exploits of a few. Jashobeam was their leader—the best of the best:

> *The first was Jashobeam the Hacmonite, who was leader of the Three—the three mightiest warriors among David's men. He once used his spear to kill 800 warriors in a single battle.*
> *—2 Samuel 23:8*

Now, not every man after God's heart will personally kill

eight hundred enemy warriors in battle, but every one of us has a supernatural potential to be extraordinary. Mighty men (and women) don't start out that way; they are made, not born. Before they were mighty, they were a mess!

*So David left Gath and escaped to the cave of Adullam. Soon his brothers and all his other relatives joined him there. Then others began coming—men who were **in trouble** or **in debt** or were just **discontented**—until David was the captain of about 400 men.*
—1 Samuel 22:1–2

Are you in debt? Are you discontent? Are you in trouble? Then you are qualified to be a mighty man! If God could help these men become mighty, He can do the same for you. In fact, our faith can have the most potential to thrive when we stand in contrast to the world rather than comfort in the world. Our society is beginning to be more openly combative in its posture toward people of faith, bringing into sharper relief the distinctions between God's ways and the world's ways. And I think that's a healthy thing for the people of God!

So stop using your circumstances as an excuse to be mediocre. Don't respond to God's call like Gideon did when "the angel of the LORD appeared to him and said, 'Mighty hero, the LORD is with you!'" (Judges 6:12). Gideon resisted this message of encouragement because he was too focused on his circumstances: "If the Lord is with us, why has all this happened to us? And where are the miracles our ancestors told us about? ... [And anyway] my clan is the weakest in the whole tribe of Manasseh, and I am the least in my entire family!" (Judges 6:13, 6:15).

Rise up, mighty warrior! Maybe you're surrounded by chaos and confusion, but God can do great things in that kind of atmosphere. Your family needs a mighty man to lead it. Your employer needs some mighty men of fortitude who will get the job done. Your church needs mighty men to follow God in faith and set the example for others, to lead them to godliness. Your God needs mighty men to stand for Him in this present evil world. Your pastor needs mighty men to fight the enemy with him, accomplishing God's will.

For the eyes of the LORD range throughout the earth to strengthen those whose hearts are fully committed to him.
—2 Chronicles 16:9 *(NIV)*

With the Lord's help, and the help of a strong brotherhood, we can all become mighty men of God! If you're still a doubter, consider Jesus' words of encouragement that cut through all excuses:

Jesus looked at them intently and said, "Humanly speaking, it is impossible. But not with God. Everything is possible with God."
—Mark 10:27

You and I cannot be mighty apart from the work of the Spirit inside of us. With Him, the impossible is manifested in and through our lives.

BECOMING A LEADER OF MIGHTY MEN

These thirty or so mighty men followed David before he was even king. It was because of David's qualities that they together rose to the height they did.

What characteristics did David possess that made him a great leader whom these mighty men would follow?

A Great Calling

Every man, but especially those of us who want to be leaders, must have a revelation of our calling to live a holy life—a life honoring God. Every one of us has a calling from God on our life, but not all of us have experienced a revelation of this yet.

> For God saved us and called us to live a holy life, not because we deserved it, but because that was his plan from before the beginning of time—to show us his grace through Christ Jesus.
> **—2 Timothy 1:9**

Though our calling is the baseline qualification, *anointing* from God for a particular role or task is the supreme qualification—preferred above education, talent, natural ability, and charm. This is why the prophet Samuel anointing young David was so significant.

Maybe you've been anointed by God for something, but you still need to be anointed by Samuel. Remember, to have authority, you must be under authority—like David served Jesse and then Saul. In the New Testament, a Roman centurion understood this spiritual concept so well, it actually amazed Jesus!

> When Jesus had entered Capernaum, a centurion came to him, asking for help. "Lord," he said, "my servant lies at home paralyzed, suffering terribly." Jesus said to him, "Shall I come and heal him?" The centurion replied, "Lord, I do not deserve to have you come under my roof. But just say the word, and my servant will be healed. For I myself am a man under authority, with soldiers under me. I tell this one, 'Go,' and he goes; and that one, 'Come,' and he comes. I say to my servant, 'Do this,' and he does it." When Jesus heard this, he was amazed and said to those following him, "Truly I tell you, I have not found anyone in Israel with such great faith."
> —*Matthew 8:5-10 (NIV)*

The centurion sensed that Jesus was operating under the authority of Another—that is, God. The mighty men of David sensed that David was operating under the authority of Another, too. There are a lot of men today claiming to be mighty, but they're not carrying the anointing needed to be great leaders of great men.

A Worthy Cause

A great leader challenges others with a great cause. Even as a youth, David had a way of making others see the cause—

standing up to the Philistines who defied the Lord God. Think about it: a little shepherd boy was able to convince the king of Israel, Saul, to let him go out and battle a giant. The king was even willing to give him his armor for the purpose!

Mighty men do not follow a great leader because the great leader said to. Mighty men follow great leaders because the great leader has presented them with a cause, a purpose, worthy of their time, talents, and efforts.

Mighty men require a God-sized purpose for their faith and courage! What we can accomplish in our own abilities isn't faith. And we might not be fighting Philistines today, but what greater cause is there than the cause of the gospel—to lead people to love God, love each other, and change the world?

Great Courage

You can't be some sniveling "momma's boy" and lead mighty men. You have to show the courage in faith that David showed even as a young shepherd.

I have done this to both lions and bears, and I'll do it to this pagan Philistine, too, for he has defied the armies of the living God! The LORD who rescued me from the claws of the lion and the bear will rescue me from this Philistine!"

Saul finally consented. "All right, go ahead," he said. "And may the LORD be with you!"
—1 Samuel 17:36–37

Mighty men sense weakness and indecision. Mighty men sense fear and cowardice. Mighty men sense a phony. And they will not follow!

It takes courage to be the kind of leader who pleases God. Sometimes that means you have to make the tough decision. You have to address what is wrong and make it right. You have to stand your ground, even when it's just you and God.

Sometimes being a courageous leader means doing the right thing even when you're facing opposition—when you're scorned, ridiculed, chastised, and gossiped about. A leader after God's own heart will stand his ground and see the matter through!

Self-discipline is the ability to do what is right even when you don't feel like doing it.

Great Character

Character creates a foundation upon which the structure of your spiritual gifts and your life can build. If there are cracks in that foundation, you can't build much before it falls down. The four pillars of character are:

Self-discipline. Self-discipline is the ability to do what is right even when you don't feel like doing it. The most important victory is to conquer self. When we give up or let ourselves live in mediocrity, our leadership will never reach its potential.

Core values. Core values give order and structure to your inner life, and when that inner life is in order, you can navigate almost anything the world throws at you. Your core values as a man after God's heart are your guiding light in life's darkest moments.

Examples include accountability, diversity, independence, simplicity, achievement, effectiveness, integrity, authority, efficiency, knowledge, structure, balance, fairness, legacy, teamwork, change, faith, loyalty, trust, commitment, family, wealth, fitness, passion, service, courage, fun, excellence, wisdom, innovation, growth, quality, honesty, and humility.

> *No matter how hard you try, you cannot consistently behave in a way that is inconsistent with how you see yourself.*

Let me give you a tip about core values: make your values God's values. Whatever your values are, make sure they line up with the heart of God and His word.

A sense of identity. No matter how hard you try, you cannot consistently behave in a way that is inconsistent with how you see yourself. Ask yourself this question: "Who am I?" Your answer is one that will drive what you do and how you act.

Integrity. Integrity is crucial for any leader. With it, leaders avoid confusion, chaos, and internal conflict.

Great Conduct

David walked out, in the flesh, what he believed. His conduct matched his character. His behavior aligned with what he believed. Mighty men don't follow hypocrites!

The truth is, people value being real over being right. But if you want to inspire and develop mighty men, you'd better start getting things right, too. Own up to it and learn when you don't, remembering what Paul wrote about standards for Christian living:

> *Above all, you must live as citizens of heaven, conducting yourselves in a manner worthy of the Good News about Christ.*
>
> **—Philippians 1:27**

Great Constraint

A great leader must constrain himself, or show great restraint. We see this in an account of the time David told the Three, captains of his mighty men, that he was thirsty:

> *David remarked longingly to his men, "Oh, how I would love some of that good water from the well by the gate in Bethlehem." So the Three broke through the Philistine lines, drew some water from the well by the gate in Bethlehem, and brought it back to David. But he refused to drink it. Instead, he poured it out as an offering to the LORD. "The LORD forbid that I should drink this!" he exclaimed. "This water is as precious as the blood of these men who risked their lives to bring it to me." So David did not drink it.*
>
> **—2 Samuel 23:15-17**

Great men follow a great leader because the leader knows how to restrain his desires. First, all his men were probably thirsty, and David knew it, so he declined to put his wants and needs before the wants and needs of those he served as a leader. Secondly, he knew the devotion and courage of the Three was far more valuable than any sip of water, and restraining his thirst was the best way to acknowledge and honor their commitment.

The capacity to restrain or control our appetites—our desires—is so vital to being a man after God's own heart, Proverbs 25:28 says that "a person without self-control is like a city with broken-down walls." Mighty men can sense broken-down walls in a leader. Let God bolster the walls of your self-control so they stand firm; others will see it and respect you more for your devotion to the Lord.

Great Commitment

What are you committed to? Your commitments shape your life. What you commit yourself to, not your past or the mistakes you make, will determine your future. And commitment makes the difference between a good leader and a great leader.

There's a difference between intentions and commitment. When you're intending to do something, you do it only when it's convenient. When you're committed to doing something, you accept no excuses, only results.

Great leaders, or kings, of mighty men have a great calling and cause. They demonstrate great character, conduct, and restraint in their actions. And they are men committed in their hearts and in their actions to serving the King of kings. From David's example, and from Jesus, we know what this looks like in practice: the good king is both humble and fully committed—like a good shepherd.

Chapter Four Questions

Question: What is your calling as a man who loves the Lord? What cause has He placed on your heart?

_____

_____

_____

_____

_____

_____

_____

_____

_____

Question: What does your conduct say about your character?

_____

_____

_____

_____

_____

_____

_____

_____

_____

Question: How does your conduct reflect your commitments?

_____

_____

_____

_____

_____

_____

_____

_____

_____

_____

_____

Action: Identify at least three specific changes you can make to your routines and habits to better align your conduct to your commitments—above all, to your commitment to the Lord. Make a specific plan for implementing these three changes. Then, begin your first step today!

Chapter Four Notes

_____

_____

_____

_____

_____

_____

_____

_____

_____

_____

_____

_____

_____

_____

_____

_____

When Sin Comes Knocking

The second most famous story of David's life, next to his battle with Goliath, was his affair with Bathsheba. The Bible sets the scene:

> *In the spring of the year, when kings normally go out to war, David sent Joab and the Israelite army to fight the Ammonites. They destroyed the Ammonite army and laid siege to the city of Rabbah. However, David stayed behind in Jerusalem. Late one afternoon, after his midday rest, David got out of bed and was walking on the roof of the palace. As he looked out over the city, he noticed a woman of unusual beauty taking a bath.*
> —*2 Samuel 11:1–2*

Before you cluck your tongue at David, remember, "if you think you are standing firm, be careful that you don't fall" (1 Corinthians 10:12 NIV). Every one of us has fallen and will fall, because we are imperfect people.

David sent someone to find out about her. The man said,
"She is Bathsheba, the daughter of Eliam and the wife of
Uriah the Hittite." Then David sent messengers to get her.
She came to him, and he slept with her. (Now she was pu-
rifying herself from her monthly uncleanness.) Then she
went back home. The woman conceived and sent word to
David, saying, "I am pregnant."

—2 Samuel 11:3–4

How did a man so on fire for God mess up so badly? By lingering over temptation to the point of forgetting about God. By making little missteps that led to bigger and bigger missteps. By failing to kill sin by running from it or resisting it.

The longer you look, the more you move in the direction of temptation.

All of us will have distractions in life, things that grab our attention and try to tempt us. The test is not if you will notice them, but if you allow yourself to linger there. The longer you look, the more you move in the direction of temptation. Looking again, and again, and again, you're moving toward the sin. This is how men get addicted to porn. David was tempted by a distraction, and he leaned into the temptation by sending out servants: first, to find out about Bathsheba, and then, to bring her to him.

Like too many men, David sacrificed his integrity, honor, and family for momentary pleasure—for a thrill. He could only do this by shoving God out of his mind as he pursued sin. The theologian Dietrich Bonhoeffer described it this way:

> At this moment God is quite unreal to us. He loses all re-
> ality, and only desire for the creature is real. The only
> reality is the devil. Satan does not here fill us with hatred
> of God, but with forgetfulness of God...[13]

When we forget about God, His calling, and His good-
ness, we're opening up a vacuum to all sorts of destructive
influences. That's what David did with Bathsheba.

Our greatest battles happen when we're bored,

not when we're busy.

LITTLE STEPS TOWARD CATASTROPHE

At a time when David should've been in a battle, he was
in the bedroom. Our greatest battles happen when we're
bored, not when we're busy. So often, we think busyness is a
bad thing. Being hurried, distracted, or overwhelmed is not
good. But being busy with good things actually *is* good! Finding something to devote your life to, to focus on, is a good
thing.

Men are like trucks: we driver better, straighter, and truer
when we're carrying a heavy load. Our most difficult times
are not when life is rough going. Hard times create dependent
people, and you don't get proud when you're dependent on
God. Survival mode, like when David was hiding in the caves,

keeps you humble. Pride, by contrast, happens when everything is swinging in your direction. When you just received that promotion—when you're growing in prestige, fame, and significance—is when you really need to watch out. Pride brings us down when people are chanting, "David, David, David!" We become prideful when we don't think we have to do what we used to do to sustain what God gave us.

David was bored. But why was David at home, wearing his royal pajamas and watching ancient SportsCenter, instead of being out on campaign like a king would normally do? Was he injured? Did he think too highly of himself? We get some insight when the Bible recounts past episodes from David's life, at the end of his life:

> *Once again the Philistines were at war with Israel. And when David and his men were in the thick of battle, David became weak and exhausted. Ishbi-benob was a descendant of the giants; his bronze spearhead weighed more than seven pounds, and he was armed with a new sword. He had cornered David and was about to kill him. But Abishai son of Zeruiah came to David's rescue and killed the Philistine. Then David's men declared, "You are not going out to battle with us again! Why risk snuffing out the light of Israel?"*
> **—2 Samuel 21:15–17**

We all know David fought the giant Goliath, but he actually fought many giants, including one named Ishbi-benob. Yet, by that point, David's age was catching up with him. The king of Israel had such a close call in his battle with Ishbi-benob, David's comrade Abishai told him, "Time out—we're not as young as we used to be. We can't run out and fight whatever battle we want, anymore. We have to be more practical now!" He didn't want the legendary king to get himself killed by refusing to accept his physical limitations.

There comes a time when every man has to face the fact that he can't do what he used to. When you're almost fifty years old, you're probably not as agile or as strong as when you were thirty. Your people don't need you to fight in the front lines of a war, at that point; you're more useful leading from a distance or on the home front, as head of your household and maybe serving in public office.

Every man can feel for David at this point. Imagine that you are known for being the giant-killer, and here you are getting bested by a giant. Your boys are looking at you saying, "You should probably stay off the battlefield from now on." Where David once found his affirmation, identity, and meaning, he was now told he wasn't good enough.

So now, all his buddies were out fighting, leaving him restless at home. And David was thinking to himself, "Man, I remember being out on campaign and sitting around the campfires. I wish I could be out there right now fighting. I miss the comradery. I wish I could still do it!"

David woke up from a nap and was walking on his rooftop, not feeling like a man anymore—and whoa, here was this woman "of unusual beauty" (in other words, she was dropdead beautiful) with no clothes on! And he said to himself. "Self, you know how to feel like a man again? If I don't get to conquer nations, maybe I can conquer women." He was resisting the need to transition into the sage phase of his life. Instead of accepting reality, he believed the lie that a relationship with a woman who was supposed to be off-limits could validate him and reaffirm his identity.

Still, nobody wakes up and says, out of nowhere, "You know what, I want to have an affair." Over the course of his life as a leader and king, David had collected wives and concubines. Each time he added a woman to his harem, he was making a poor decision on a small scale that ultimately made it easier for him to commit sin and tragedy on a massive scale.

> And he became more and more powerful, because the LORD God Almighty was with him. Now Hiram king of Tyre sent envoys to David, along with cedar logs and carpenters and stonemasons, and they built a palace for David. Then David knew that the LORD had established him as king over Israel and had exalted his kingdom for the sake of his people Israel. After he left Hebron, David took more concubines and wives in Jerusalem, and more sons and daughters were born to him.
> **—2 Samuel 5:10–13**

The passion of sex is not satisfied by a full harem of women; it is increased. The lie of worldly culture is that to soothe your sex drive, you must satisfy it. The truth? The more you satisfy it, the more it increases. Little acts of poor judgment pave the way to catastrophe in our lives. And taking many wives was, indeed, an act of poor judgment and disobedience on David's part. God had warned His people about the danger of this:

> When you enter the land the LORD your God is giving you and have taken possession of it and settled in it, and you

say, "Let us set a king over us like all the nations around us," be sure to appoint over you a king the LORD your God chooses. He must be from among your fellow Israelites. Do not place a foreigner over you, one who is not an Israelite. The king, moreover, must not acquire great numbers of horses for himself or make the people return to Egypt to get more of them, for the LORD has told you, "You are not to go back that way again." He must not take many wives, or his heart will be led astray. He must not accumulate large amounts of silver and gold.
—Deuteronomy 17:14–17

David was vulnerable because of his stage in life, and he was unaccountable because of his status as king. Like so many others, he was an unfinished man. Those small bad decisions, added up, would lead to increasingly catastrophic decisions.

HIDDEN CONSEQUENCES

His initial cover-up plan was to trick Uriah into taking a break from the war to spend the night with his wife. Then, when Bathsheba started to show her pregnancy, she could say, "Oh look, Uriah, you're a daddy!" And hopefully, no one would notice that Uriah Jr. looked a lot like David.

When Satan tempts, he never

presents the consequences.

But when Uriah proved to be too dedicated a soldier to play along with David's plan, David conspired with one of his generals to leave Uriah stranded in the thick of the fighting. This loyal warrior was left hanging out to dry by the shameful secret order of his king. And remember, Uriah wasn't just some foot soldier; he was one of the original men who went to David in the cave and came to be numbered among the Thirty, David's mighty men. David had let boredom and pride turn him into a traitor to one of his most committed followers, his brother in arms.

> *When Uriah's wife heard that her husband was dead, she mourned for him. After the time of mourning was over, David had her brought to his house, and she became his wife and bore him a son. But the thing David had done displeased the LORD.*
> *—2 Samuel 11:26–27*

This backup plan worked, and David thought he had gotten away with it. But of course, God was not happy about it. How could a man after God's own heart have fallen so low?

When Satan tempts, he never presents the consequences. He will only show you the excitement, the thrill, and the fun, but he will never tell you what comes further down the road of this decision.

Satan doesn't want the heavy drinker to think about how he'll feel worse the next morning, or how he could lose his family and career to the habit. And when the opportunity for extramarital indiscretions come along, the enemy urges, "Go ahead and sleep with her. You deserve it, and she's obviously into you." Satan doesn't tell a man filled with lust about the pregnancy that's coming or the broken families that will result. "Go ahead and watch porn," he whispers, failing to mention that pornography twists a man's heart and mind with arousal and leads him to chase women who aren't committed to doing life God's way. There are always consequences, and here were David's:

> This is what the LORD says: "Out of your own household I am going to bring calamity on you. Before your very eyes I will take your wives and give them to one who is close to you, and he will sleep with your wives in broad daylight. You did it in secret, but I will do this thing in broad daylight before all Israel. ... [B]ecause by doing this you have shown utter contempt for the LORD, the son born to you will die."
> —*2 Samuel 12:11–12, 12:13*

God still loved David, but David's sin would bring loss, grief, embarrassment, and division to his family. And it seems like Solomon, David's second son with Bathsheba, observed how his father treated women, because he would grow up to show similar weakness in that area of his life. As great and wise a king as Solomon became, he displayed the same false masculinity as David when it came to women. The harem of wives and concubines Solomon accumulated brought foreign idols into his household (1 Kings 11), which led not only the king himself but all Israel astray. When we listen to Satan, and to our pride, it's never worth it.

HOW TO KILL SIN

Be killing sin, or it will be killing you.
—**John Owen**[14]

Sometimes, it can seem simpler and easier to face a giant on the battlefield than to confront our sins. How do we kill our sins?

Run

David had the opportunity to turn and run, right at the start:

> *He sent someone to find out who she was, and he was told, "She is Bathsheba, the daughter of Eliam and the wife of Uriah the Hittite."*
>
> *—2 Samuel 11:3*

This report—slipping in the bit about Bathsheba being the wife of one of David's most loyal warriors—was a subtle warning of wisdom, but it didn't even register to David. At this moment, to borrow Bonhoeffer's words, God was "quite unreal" to David. Those small bad decisions, added up, will lead to a catastrophic decision.

When dealing with temptation, sin, and the devil's lies, "fight the good fight" (1 Timothy 6:12). Like Paul wrote to the Ephesians, "Put on all of God's armor so that you will be able to stand firm against all strategies of the devil" (Ephesians 6:11). You need to strap on "the belt of truth," "the body armor of God's righteousness," the peace of the gospel, "the shield of faith," the helmet of salvation, and "the sword of the Spirit, which is the Word of God" (Ephesians 6:14–17). Know that the battle belongs to the Lord and "we are more than conquerors" in our reliance on Christ (Romans 8:37 NIV).

Don't flirt with temptation. Flee from temptation.

But you want to know what the Bible says about sexual immorality? Flee! *Run.*

> *Flee from sexual immorality. All other sins a man commits are outside his body, but he who sins sexually sins against his own body.*
> **—1 Corinthians 6:18**

Don't flirt with temptation. Flee from temptation. If you don't run, you will fall. Our culture has become so immersed in sensuality, most people have become desensitized to concepts of sexual morality and immorality related to marriage. If you think your marriage is "just a piece of paper," realize that no, it's not the ink that makes a difference in relationships between men and women. The blessing of God is what makes the difference.

And when God tells us to do something, it's not that He doesn't want us to have fun or He's a prude. He doesn't want our lives destroyed. When we tell our children not to play in the street, it's not because we don't want them to have fun; we want to save their lives so, among other things, they *can* have fun. We want them to be around, alive, long enough to have fun. The reason God commands us to flee from sexual immorality is because it opens the door to so many other sins.

God's instructions for us about sexual morality are guard rails to keep us from driving off the side of a mountain. For David, like for so many men and women before and since, sexual immorality started with adultery and led to deception, manipulation, and many other evils. It will lead to the crumbling of your marriage and the ruin of your life if you don't man up and run.

Resist

So the question becomes, "What are you actively doing to try to keep sin from happening?" What blocks do you have on your computer or your phone?

What safety measures do you have when you see what you didn't even seek out to see? Who are your accountability partners? We need to use wisdom and steer clear of sexual temptation:

> *Keep to a path far from her, do not go near the door of her house.*
> **—Proverbs 5:8**

As a side note, the fact that Bathsheba was bathing naked on a rooftop in sight of the king's palace does raise some questions. Of course, the answers to those questions don't excuse David, either way. Bathsheba might not have helped, and she participated in the adultery, but David was the instigator. He had failed to put sufficient precautions in place or to allow himself to be held accountable.

Repent

David, the man after God's heart, tried to hide his sin for a long time. The sweet singer of Israel was now living a lie, faking his existence in a minor key, and he suffered for it. David sang:

> *When I refused to confess my sin, my body wasted away, and I groaned all day long. Day and night your hand of discipline was heavy on me. My strength evaporated like water in the summer heat.*
>
> **—Psalm 32:3-4**

God sent Nathan the prophet to confront David and bring into the light the thing that was eating him up in the dark.

> *Then David said to Nathan, "I have sinned against the* LORD.*" Nathan replied, "The* LORD *has taken away your sin. You are not going to die."*
>
> **—2 Samuel 12:13**

We can't care what other people, public opinion, or social media say is good, natural, or acceptable behavior. We have to recognize when we've violated the God-created order of things and sinned against Him. When we take off the mask and come into the light, God washes and purifies us, forgiving us.

111

Refocus

Sin has consequences, but we are not condemned to live in our past mistakes. David suffered the consequences and then *got up* off the ground, renewed.

> *On the seventh day the child died. ...Then David got up from the ground. After he had washed, put on lotions and changed his clothes, he went into the house of the LORD and worshiped.*
> **—2 Samuel 12:18, 12:20**

Today, like David, make a fresh commitment to spiritual, moral, ethical, and sexual purity. God expects a man after His own heart to recognize when to get up off the ground and refocus on Him. As men, our families, churches, and communities need us to lead by example when we've fallen short. We can do this because we are made righteous, finished, and whole in Him.

Chapter Five Questions

Question: What is a sin or temptation you've frequently struggled with? Why do you think this has been a particular struggle for you?

_____

_____

_____

_____

_____

_____

_____

_____

Question: How does this sin or temptation try to distract you from God? What are the hidden consequences of choosing to pursue that path?

_____

_____

_____

_____

_____

_____

_____

_____

Question: How can you establish better accountability for yourself in the area of this sin?

_____

_____

_____

_____

_____

_____

_____

_____

_____

_____

_____

_____

Action: What is your plan to kill this sin that's been a giant challenge in your life? Depending on what this sin is doing, or trying to do, in your life right now, what will it look like for you to run, to resist, to repent, and/or to refocus?

Chapter Five Notes

_____

_____

_____

_____

_____

_____

_____

_____

_____

_____

_____

_____

_____

_____

_____

Healing the Father Wound

Jens Johnnie Pulver, known as Lil Evil, was a five-foot, seven-inch UFC Champion. He also became a Christian later in life and wrote an autobiography,[15] in which he told the story of his relationship with his father.

This brutally tough fighter had grown up under the worst of circumstances, including an incident in which his dad put a gun in seven-year-old Jens's mouth—before pulling away because, he claimed, his son wasn't worth a bullet.

Many years later, after winning a championship title, he broke down crying and said, on national television, "See, Dad? I did amount to something!"

Pulver was fighting his dad—punching him, beating on him—every time he climbed into the ring. He spent his whole life raging against his old man. Like many other men, he had a father wound.

The concept of the father wound is so significant for understanding your heart and your soul. A father wound cuts deep.

David had a lot of successes, but because of some of his choices, especially his adultery with Bathsheba and the murderous aftermath, he and his family faced consequences. Yes, David repented and got right with God, but some of those consequences remained, including father wounds.

> *Do not be deceived: God cannot be mocked. A man reaps what he sows. Whoever sows to please their flesh, from the flesh will reap destruction; whoever sows to please the Spirit, from the Spirit will reap eternal life.*
> **—Galatians 6:7–8**

If you sow a seed in the natural, natural consequences will ensue. Physical sin has physical consequences, emotional sin leads to emotional consequences, and so on. But amid the consequences of his sin, David didn't wallow in his failure. He was broken before God but then refocused on God, and this is what made him a man after God's own heart.

> *The consequences of an untreated father wound can lead people down the road to all kinds of addictions and dysfunctions.*

WANDERING INTO THE WOODS

David's first child with Bathsheba was the son who died in infancy, and she later gave birth to the future king, Solomon. But we've read that David had many other wives and concubines, so he had many other sons and daughters. A family feud between David and one of those sons, Absalom, divided Israel. A wedge of unforgiveness had split the kingdom between a father and his son, who bore a father wound.

Everyone who has ever felt disapproval, rejection, or abandonment from his or her father has a wound like this. The consequences of an untreated father wound can lead people down the road to all kinds of addictions and dysfunctions. Prisons across the nation are filled with people whose common denominator is that they carry a father wound that never healed; they never found forgiveness. Even in the best home, there is opportunity for wounds to be inflicted and to fester.

David's household wasn't exactly the best home. Absalom developed a father wound, nursed the wound, and eventually took his dad to war.

David's army marched out of the city to fight Israel, and the battle took place in the forest of Ephraim.
—2 Samuel 18:6–9

There is a war happening in our homes, too. We may not be facing giants or Philistines. Amalekites and Hittites might not be coming against you and your family. But make no mistake: just because we can't see the enemy crawling in our window and breaking down our door doesn't mean we aren't under siege! Our enemy is clever and strategic, and our war against him is for our family, our identity, and our soul. It's a fight for masculinity in a culture that endorses turning men into women and women into men. The world confuses men into not knowing who they are or how to function. There is a war to wage, but many of us are not dressed properly for it. For spiritual battle, Ephesians 6:10–17 tells us, we are to put on the armor of God: truth, righteousness, the peace of the gospel, faith, salvation, and the Word of God.

In the physical war between the king and his son, David's loyalists beat back Absalom's army: "There was a great slaughter that day, and 20,000 men laid down their lives. The battle raged all across the countryside, and more men died because of the forest than were killed by the sword" (2 Samuel 18:7–8).

Can you imagine walking into the forest and seeing twenty thousand corpses strewn everywhere, strung over branches, roots, and stumps? These bodies didn't show normal kinds of wounds, from swords or spears, but they were dead all the same. And this wasn't some fantastical forest of bad-tempered trees or walking, talking tree-folk who shuffled around tearing up armies of baddies, like in Tolkien's *Lord of the Rings*. These were just normal trees, but God used them to hand David the victory.

In our world today, though, it's the enemy trying to pull you off the battlefield and into the woods of discouragement, bitterness, and secret sin. These woods represent anything that is not God's plan for your life. But unlike Absalom's warriors, we have the armor we need to win our battles in the forest. We must do everything it takes to win the fight, but we have guaranteed victory in Christ.

During his battle with David's men, Absalom himself

wandered into the woods, too:

Now Absalom happened to meet David's men. He was riding his mule, and as the mule went under the thick branches of a large oak, Absalom's hair got caught in the tree. He was left hanging in midair, while the mule he was riding kept on going.

—*2 Samuel 18:9*

As men, we're meant to be leaders. So, we have to realize, if we wander into the woods of sin, other people are following us. We shouldn't deceive ourselves for a second that our sin doesn't affect our family.

Maybe you tell yourself that because you do things in secret, it won't transfer to your children and your spouse, but the truth is, people are following you into those woods. Worse, they may lose themselves deeper in the forest than you do. You may think there's no harm in getting a little lost in drink—you tell yourself you can handle it—but maybe your spouse or child notices, follows you down that road, and develops an addiction.

In the end, Absalom "was left hanging in midair," by his hair, from a tree. Here's my point: the devil is not in a hurry to pierce your heart if he's caught you by your head. If the enemy owns your eyes, your ears, and your mind, why does he need to bother killing you?

Let's look at what led Absalom to this place. Maybe exploring the story of his father wound will shed some light on aspects of *your* story.

CAUSES OF THE FATHER WOUND

It had started almost ten years prior. Everything seemed to be going well enough in David's palace, although with so many wives and children living in one household, friction and rivalries were inevitable. One day, David's son Amnon did something evil: he sexually defiled his half-sister Tamar, who happened to be Absalom's sister (2 Samuel 13). And this terrible offense caused a rift in the family because David didn't know what to do.

> *When King David heard what had happened, he was very angry.*
> *—2 Samuel 13:21*

As far as I can tell, David was being a classic passive dad here. He got mad, but there was no follow-through. Why didn't David step in to correct and rebuke Amnon directly? Why didn't David discipline his son for his wicked behavior? *What was David thinking?*

Sometimes, we put dads and leaders on pedestals and assume they will always know what to do. It's important to remember that no one gets it right all the time. There are no perfect fathers on earth; there is only one perfect Father up above. Yet the mistakes we make when we don't rely on godly wisdom and truth have very real consequences for us and those around us.

In this case, David messed up big. He missed the mark.

And because he missed it, Tamar's brother Absalom grew bitter and angry, to the point where he hated not only Amnon but also their father, David, who had failed to confront Amnon's evil act in a substantive way. Internally, Absalom burned with hatred, and this father wound only worsened as he gave Amnon, and probably David as well, the silent treatment for two years (2 Samuel 13:22–23).

Salvation makes us new creations in Christ, yet it does not necessarily address this wound inside. You can be forgiven but remain broken.

Then, one day, Absalom conspired to murder Amnon in revenge. So much for time healing all wounds. Then Absalom fled and lived far away from his father for three years (2 Samuel 13:37–38), until David called him back home:

> So the king sent for Joab and told him, "All right, go and bring back the young man Absalom." ... But the king gave this order: "Absalom may go to his own house, but he must never come into my presence." So Absalom did not see the king.
> —*2 Samuel 14:21, 14:24*

David refused to let his son see his face. Absalom could live nearby, but David denied him his father's presence. Absalom wasn't allowed to have a relationship with his dad, even though they lived in the same neighborhood again. This wasn't just a highly volatile situation, awkward for everyone involved, and prime material for an ancient Israelite soap opera. It was also emotionally and spiritually unhealthy.

The father wound is the absence of love from your birth father. This wound can be caused by:

- Neglect that leaves you thinking, "I am unimportant."

- Absence as a result of divorce, separation, or death. Your father simply wasn't there.

- Abuse, whether mental, physical, sexual, or spiritual. When you wanted a hug, you received a hit.

- Control of a father who was oppressive, overpowering, and domineering.

- Withholding of love or affirmation. Maybe you never heard your dad simply say, "I love you."

Salvation makes us new creations in Christ, yet it does not necessarily address this wound inside. You can be forgiven but remain broken. The effects of a father wound are low self-esteem, a deep emotional pain inside, and a performance orientation that makes us "human doings" rather than "human beings."

Twenty-four million children in America right now are growing up without a father figure in their life. Between first grade and twelfth grade, 21 percent of kids don't have a father figure.[16] They don't have a father who believes in them and says, "I love you." They don't have a father's validation and affirmation. Women with a father wound can develop a negative filter obscuring their view of men. They may have trust issues and be terrified of abandonment. And they may fall in love with father-wounded men.

Despite his hatred, Absalom was craving a father in his life. Even those of us who grew up in the best homes can relate: we have experienced wounds when our dad didn't show up or when he didn't tell us we'd done a good job. A father's silence speaks volumes. When you were hoping he was going to say, "I'm proud of you," maybe he said, "I'm disappointed in you." And maybe when you were hoping he was going to hug you, he walked away instead.

Over time, these little wounds can accumulate. If we don't know who to take them to, or where to open up—if we close up and content ourselves with ear-tickling sermons—we miss out on the healing that our Father God wants to bring into our hearts. We're unfinished men, but with His healing, we can be the men and women of God, the fathers and mothers, He has called us to be.

Time won't heal what you won't face.

BARRIERS TO HEALING

Untreated wounds can persist for decades, causing ongoing hurt in our lives and the lives of those around us. With that in mind, let's address some of the barriers that inhibit the healing of our father wounds.

Pride

The sinful character trait of pride inhibits us from having the will to confront our wound or change our attitude toward it. "I'm all right," you tell yourself and other people. "The wounds happened a long time ago, you know. We don't talk about it, and that works for me." Again, the notion that time will heal all wounds is baloney. Time won't heal what you won't face. Absalom waited for years, and the wound only influenced him more, driving him to the wicked act of killing his half-brother.

Absalom's revenge-murder of Amnon points to another symptom of pride: thinking that we're so important, there's no way to deal with an offense against us except for returning the offense. In pride, we believe we have to give as good as we got, making our own justice.

And boy, was Absalom a man filled with pride. In case we missed that, the Bible tells us how ridiculously vain he was about his hair:

> Now Absalom was praised as the most handsome man in all Israel. He was flawless from head to foot. He cut his hair only once a year, and then only because it was so heavy. When he weighed it out, it came to five pounds! ... Absalom lived in Jerusalem for two years, but he never got to see the king.
> —*2 Samuel 14:25–28*

This man was the Fabio, the Bieber, maybe the Zoolander, of Israel in his day: he was a good-looking guy, and he and everyone else knew it. Apparently, he turned his annual haircut into a national event, where his glorious mane was cut and weighed while the crowd looked on. It was absurd.

But no matter how good he looked, how much attention he garnered, or how hard he tried to get his dad's approval, he didn't receive it. I'm sure Absalom had sought a father's validation from David his whole life, but he never received it. Holding onto that injured pride only deepened his wound.

The Holy Spirit brings you to Jesus for forgiveness so He can introduce you to your Father for your healing.

Deception

Misconceptions about the self, our birth father, and our Father God are also common barriers to healing. When we hold a concept of our birth father as angry, violent, uncaring, indifferent, distant, withdrawn, absent, abandoning, alcoholic, condemning, or critical, we tend to believe the following lies about ourselves:

- "I am unworthy."

- "I am stupid."

- "I am incompetent."

- "I am unloved or unlovable."

As long as we accept these misconceptions as truth, we

will experience depressed, anxious, angry lives. But there was an even bigger reason the enemy targeted your dad, and it wasn't just to ruin your relationship. The enemy wants to destroy the relationship between you and your heavenly Father.

Often, a person's image of God the Father is contaminated by his personal experience with his birth father.

Maybe you love Jesus but it's hard for you to relate to God the Father. You can say wholeheartedly, "I love Jesus," but how often do you say with conviction, "I love you, Father"? You love the story where the Son is the hero, but the Father stays in the background.

Jesus said, "No man can come to the Father except through me" (John 14:6). Jesus' job is to get you to your Dad in heaven. The Holy Spirit brings you to Jesus for forgiveness so He can introduce you to your Father for your healing. Yet, you can be forgiven and choose to stay broken, putting up barriers against the healing God offers.

Often, a person's image of God the Father is contaminated by his personal experience with his birth father. When misconceptions about God are present—for instance, that He is angry, judgmental, displeased, fearsome, legalistic, quick to punish, and slow to forgive—the false words we tend to believe are:

- "I am not good enough."
- "I am guilty and shameful."

- "I must work harder to justify myself."

These deceptions will creep into our life, and we'll find ourselves lying or manipulating facts, even manipulating people, to get what we want. Denied the approval of his father, Absalom decided it would be better to get rid of David. He began to curry favor with the people of Israel, fostering a spirit of rebellion against his father.

After this, Absalom bought a chariot and horses, and he hired fifty bodyguards to run ahead of him. He got up early every morning and went out to the gate of the city. When people brought a case to the king for judgment, Absalom would ask where in Israel they were from, and they would tell him their tribe. Then Absalom would say, "You've really got a strong case here! It's too bad the king doesn't have anyone to hear it. I wish I were the judge. Then everyone could bring their cases to me for judgment, and I would give them justice!" When people tried to bow before him, Absalom wouldn't let them. Instead, he took them by the hand and kissed them. Absalom did this with everyone who came to the king for judgment, and so he stole the hearts of all the people of Israel.
—2 Samuel 15:1–6

God never honors dishonor, and He never blesses a spirit of rebellion.

The Wound

The wound itself, nursing the continuous emotional hurt inside, can cause our hearts to become calloused. Jesus said:

For this people's heart has become calloused; they hardly hear with their ears, and they have closed their eyes. Otherwise they might see with their eyes, hear with their ears, understand with their hearts and turn, and I would heal them.

—**Matthew 13:15**

When we shut our eyes and ears to the truth of our identity in Christ and the loving nature of God our Father, we close off our hearts to His healing presence in our father wounds.

HEALING THE FATHER WOUND

How do we overcome these barriers and allow God to heal us of our father wounds? It begins with admitting our wounds exist.

Before you can begin to forgive a father, you must first realize and acknowledge the ways you have been wounded by him.

Realization

You can't address a problem you don't know exists. "You can't heal a wound by saying it's not there!" (Jeremiah 6:14 TLB). You can't heal what you keep buried.

A wounded girl who ignores the problem turns into a wounded woman. The wounded boy grows into a wounded man. And wounded people may say they're fine, but all the

130

while, they're bleeding on people who didn't hurt them. Before you can begin to forgive a father, you must first realize and acknowledge the ways you have been wounded by him.

> *For I am afflicted and needy, and my heart is wounded within me.*
> —*Psalm 109:22* (NASB)

Grieving this gives you an opportunity to weep over what's been lost: time, innocence, relationships, childhood, and peace.

Now, after realization, there is a tendency for suppression. It's like deleting a bunch of storage on your computer but never emptying the trash. Just because the garbage isn't on your desktop anymore doesn't mean it isn't taking up space.

Lead from your scars, not your wounds.

Transformation

Invite Jesus into your wounds. In the healing process, the wound becomes a scar, which might not look pretty. But a scar, at least, is a wound that has healed. We need to bring our wounds to Jesus, let Him heal them, and use our scars for Jesus. Our scars may be our greatest ministry.

Lead from your scars, not your wounds. I don't want to preach wounded! If I preach wounded, I will inflict my pain on you. I don't want to be a wounded pastor, parent, or spouse. Wounded me doesn't have to hold me down forever, but I have to let God transform my wounds into scars.

This is something I love about Jesus: He got up out of the grave, but He kept the scars of His suffering. That fact gives us hope. We should also take courage from knowing we're not healed through our own effort, achievement, or strength:

> *By His wounds you have been healed.*
> **—1 Peter 2:24**

One of the big challenges of the father wound is constantly feeling we have to earn our healing. But a whole person works *from* his identity not *for* his identity. God didn't create us to be achievers, but to be receivers. Our identity is something we receive from Him. Through Christ, we receive righteousness and our adoption into God's family. On our own, we can't achieve any of that.

Transformation happens when we invite Jesus into our wounds and our memories: "Let God transform you into a new person by changing the way you think" (Romans 12:2). Be careful not to invite any other influences into the wound in your heart. Understand the words spoken over your life and identify the source of every thought you allow to mark you. "We take captive every thought to make it obedient to Christ" (2 Corinthians 10:5), and that's how we let the Lord turn our wounds into scars.

Confrontation

Forgive your father. A common misconception about forgiveness is that it requires you to excuse or dismiss the actions of your offender. Dismissal is not forgiveness, nor is it a healthy way to process pain.

When we cling to resentment like Absalom did, it causes us to remain stuck: forever the child, forever the victim. The longer we hold on to unforgiveness, the longer the pain will control our life. To quote Nelson Mandela, "When a deep injury has been done to us, we never heal until we forgive."[17] And to quote Paul:

> Get rid of all bitterness, rage, anger, harsh words, and slander, as well as all types of evil behavior. Instead, be kind to each other, tenderhearted, forgiving one another, just as God through Christ has forgiven you.
> **—Ephesians 4:31–32**

Bitterness, anger, and unforgiveness will block the healing of our father wounds. So confront the source of your wound—face your father, whatever that looks like in your situation—and forgive him. Hand over your bitterness to God and be healed.

Restoration

Healing requires us to accept God's truth about ourselves—and He says we're His adopted children!

So you have not received a spirit that makes you fearful slaves. Instead, you received God's Spirit when He adopted you as His own children. Now we call Him, "Abba, Father."
—Romans 8:15

In place of misconceptions and lies, receive these words of truth about yourself from our heavenly Dad:

- "I am accepted." (Romans 8:34)

- "I am chosen." (1 Peter 2:9)

- "I am loved." (1 John 4:16)

- "I am God's creation." (Colossians 1:16)

- "I am precious in His sight." (Isaiah 43:4)

- "I am forgiven." (1 John 1:9)

- "I have been redeemed." (Ephesians 1:7)

- "I will never be left or forsaken." (Hebrews 13:5)

- "I have an eternal inheritance." (1 Peter 1:4)

- "Nothing can separate me from the love of God." (Romans 8:38)

To truly heal from a father wound, you must restore God's narrative about yourself and your worth. Embrace Him as your perfect Father:

"And I will be your Father, and you will be my sons and daughters", says the Lord Almighty.
—2 Corinthians 6:18

Chapter Six Questions

Question: What father wound do you carry? What were the causes of this wound?

_____

_____

_____

_____

_____

_____

_____

_____

_____

Question: How has your father wound affected your life? How has your wound affected your family and others around you?

_____

_____

_____

_____

_____

_____

_____

_____

_____

Question: What barriers have you faced to healing your father wound?

_____

_____

_____

_____

_____

_____

_____

_____

_____

Action: At this point in your life, what steps do you need to take to heal your father wound? Whom do you need to forgive, and how can you demonstrate that forgiveness? What is your next step to healing?

Chapter Six Notes

Leaving a Legacy

After seventy years, David's life was coming to a close, but he would be remembered as a great king. Along with his son Solomon, he would become known as one of the greatest kings ever to reign in Israel or Judah. He oversaw the development and enlargement of the kingdom and the empowerment of his people. Lapses in judgment and moments of serious sin aside, David displayed passion for, and wholehearted devotion to, God throughout his life.

You might have messed up,

but you can still leave a legacy.

Listen, by the time you reach the sage stage of masculinity, you will have made mistakes, too—a lot of them. You might have messed up, but you can still leave a legacy. The final test of David's life was raising up the next king of Israel. And God saw it fit to choose his surviving son with Bathsheba:

Solomon. Isn't that like God, to take our most embarrassing mistake and turn it around for his glory?

David took this transcribed prayer of Moses and included it in the Psalms:

> *Teach us to number our days, that we may gain a heart of wisdom.*
> **—Psalm 90:12**

He knew that awareness of our mortality and our limitations opens our hearts to wise perspectives. Part of wisdom is an awareness of what we'll leave behind when we die—that is, our legacy.

As a pastor, visiting people in hospitals and attending funerals, I've heard a lot of life stories. Sometimes these stories have made me think, "What will my family say when I'm gone? What will my friends say when I leave?" What will you leave when you leave?

WHAT WILL YOU LEAVE WHEN YOU LEAVE?

In 1 Chronicles 28 and 29, David brought together all the leaders of Israel, and his son Solomon, to offer some final words:

> *And Solomon, my son, learn to know the God of your ancestors intimately. Worship and serve him with your whole heart and a willing mind. For the Lord sees every heart and knows every plan and thought. If you seek him, you will find him. But if you forsake him, he will reject you forever.*
> **—1 Chronicles 28:9**

The three things David told Solomon were:

Know God intimately. You can't survive on your father's faith. You need your own relationship with the Lord.

Serve Him with a willing mind and spirit. In the Hebrew, "willing" was *chaphets*—meaning, to take pleasure or delight in something, to be inclined to do something, or to bend toward something or someone.[18] Willingness means to do something because we want to and therefore choose to. The Lord knows our willingness because He searches our heart.

Serve Him wholeheartedly. In the Hebrew, "wholeheartedly" is *shalem*—meaning, "unhewn" or untouched stones.[19] The temple God commanded Solomon to build would be with *shalem*, uncut stone, representing an "uncut" heart: wholehearted devotion.

You see, whether you're the king of Israel or a shepherd, a CEO or an hourly employee, we're all fighting the same battle over our heart. What we leave behind when we leave is determined by this: how much of our heart did God get?

At the end of the fight, how much of our heart was truly God's territory? How much of our heart did we cede to our own selfish desires, or to our desire for others' approval? How much was left for God? The answer to that question shapes our legacy.

DEFINING *LEGACY*

I love the word *legacy*. I want to examine this word and concept more closely before we continue to study David's final words and actions as king. Legacy boils down to what people remember when we're gone. There's going to be a day when you will leave this earth. What will people talk about at your memorial service? What will you have left behind for them?

Those who are righteous will be remembered forever.
—Psalm 112:6

Righteousness doesn't mean being perfect in your own actions; it means you decided to choose the right path through Jesus, and it is *He* who makes you righteous. We trust in Him and commit ourselves to living life for Him: "I'm going to live my life right—because, Jesus!" It's the people who decide to live right who don't just get talked about for a few moments in a service. No, they are remembered forever.

What we do for ourselves usually dies with us. What we do for others lives beyond us.

You might say, "Jason, if we're living for the Lord, does it really matter what people say about us? Is that the sort of motivation we should care about?" Sure, wanting people to speak well of you isn't the primary motivation, but it's a fine secondary motivation to have, if Jesus comes first.

When God created us, He put endorphins inside of us, chemicals that are released when we're generous so that we would experience pleasure and delight when making a difference in other people's lives.[20] God did that on purpose so we would have some added incentive not to sit around and only take care of ourselves.

God is not unjust; he will not forget your work [your outreach efforts, the big tip you gave your server, and so on] and the love you have shown him as you have helped his people and continue to help them.
—Hebrews 6:10

Even secular academic theorists like Abraham Maslow have suggested that the highest degree of human motivation and functioning is self-transcendence,[21] which includes living beyond ourselves and leaving a legacy. But we know legacy is not just about what people remember; it's also about what *God* remembers when we're gone from this earth.

We're not just in a race; we're in a relay.

Why does God put that motivation inside us to consider others, and why does He reward us when we act on it? Because otherwise, we probably wouldn't! We all have a gravitational pull toward selfishness. You leave Jason Hanash alone for long enough, without the Word of God and the leading of the Holy Spirit, and—well, I am a selfish human being. We forget!

What we do for ourselves usually dies with us. What we do for others lives beyond us. David is remembered as a great king not because of his achievements, but because of what people and God remembered about him when he was gone. It wasn't what he did for himself that was remembered, but what he did for the Lord and for others.

This is how the good news of the gospel spreads: people serving the interests of God and other people. Jesus was counting on us leaving a legacy when He entrusted us with the mission of making disciples and advancing the gospel:

> And the things you have heard me say in the presence of
> many witnesses entrust to reliable people who will also be
> qualified to teach others.
>
> —*2 Timothy 2:2* (NIV)

We were never meant to just hoard things of value, whether it's the resources of this world, the wisdom of the Word of God, or the gifts of the Spirit. We're not meant to accumulate it, but to pass it on. See, we're not just in a race; we're in a relay. The baton David was passing was his passion for God. The greatest investment in your life is not an IRA or 401K—it's people! People outlast buildings. People outlast companies. People outlast financial resources. The best investment David made was not in the building of the temple; it was in Solomon himself.

You can't control the legacy you receive, but you can control the legacy you leave.

Again, what will people say at your funeral? On one hand, I've been at funerals where people don't know what to say, and they're trying hard to find something, anything, positive. On the other hand, I've been at other funerals where you couldn't stop people from sharing. Why? Because in those cases, the deceased person had made an impact on others' lives.

What baton are you passing in your relay? Many of us were not even handed the baton from our father. The baton I received was dropped and dirty when I took it up. I was living on food stamps with a single mom, surrounded by addiction and violence. Listen to me, man of God: you can't control the legacy you receive, but you can control the legacy you leave! Pick up your baton and pass on something better.

David couldn't control the legacy he received from his

dad, either. From his example, we see that even if we've messed up, and even if we didn't have the best role models growing up, we can still man up and leave a valuable legacy.

Legacy people have an eternal mindset.

A LEGACY LIFE

Imagine you have one last hour to live, so you bring your kids together for one final conversation. You have to hustle. The kids file in and look at you expectantly. Some might just be wondering who gets your money, but you know what's most important: it's time to drop some godly wisdom.

An Eternal Mindset

Legacy people have an eternal mindset. We see this perspective reflected in the last words of David to his son:

> *As the time of King David's death approached, he gave this charge to his son Solomon: "**I am going where everyone on earth must someday go**. Take courage and be a man. Observe the requirements of the Lord your God, and follow all his ways. Keep the decrees, commands, regulations, and laws written in the Law of Moses so that you will be successful in all you do and wherever you go."*
> *—1 Kings 2:1–3*

I did the research: one out of one people dies. But we don't have to fear death, because Jesus conquered it; now, it has no power or hold on us. Thanks to Jesus, we have eternal homes in heaven! You can make all the money in the world, but if you don't know where your eternal destination is, you can gain the whole world and still lose your soul (Matthew 16:26). What's the point in that?

David wasn't concerned with just leaving Solomon resources, but with leaving a legacy.

Legacy people see this life on earth through the lens of eternity. They understood Jesus' message: "You're going to have to focus on Me! Discipline your eyes not to just look around for opportunities to benefit you or problems that threaten you. Instead, keep your eyes on the harvest of souls for God's kingdom!"

I tell you, open your eyes and look at the fields! They are ripe for harvest.
—John 4:35

Incidentally, I've never seen a U-Haul behind a hearse. All of our stuff is going to be gone, out of reach, when we depart this life; we can't take it with us. David wasn't concerned with just leaving Solomon resources, but with leaving a legacy.

So we don't look at the troubles we can see now; rather, we fix our gaze on things that cannot be seen. For the things we see now will soon be gone, but the things we cannot see will last forever.

—2 Corinthians 4:18

The goal isn't to live on earth forever, but to leave something that does endure beyond us.

"Things we cannot see"—what falls into this category? Yes, the work of God's kingdom includes what God is doing in children's ministries and in small groups. It includes teens giving their testimony in youth group and having life-changing conversations with their mentors. It's about hands flying up in surrender to Jesus.

And it's also about the less visible things, like the healing of a father wound and somebody truly embracing God as Father for the first time in their life. These are eternal things. The goal isn't to live on earth forever, but to leave something that endures beyond us.

No one makes a difference without giving up something.

Willingness to Sacrifice

Legacy people understand sacrifice. I've come to this conclusion: no one makes a difference without giving up something.

Now David assembled at Jerusalem all the officials of Is-
rael, the leaders of the tribes, and the commanders of the
divisions that served the king, the commanders of thou-
sands, and the commanders of hundreds, and the overseers
of all the property and livestock belonging to the king and
his sons, with the officials and the mighty men, all the val-
iant warriors.

—1 Chronicles 28:1 *(NASB)*

Can you imagine that scene? The gathering of all those
high-ranking servants was impressive and dramatic, and it
was a testament to the respect and loyalty David commanded.

Then King David rose to his feet and said, "Listen to me, my
brothers and my people; I had intended to build a perma-
nent home for the ark of the covenant of the LORD and for
the footstool of our God. So I had made preparations to
build it. But God said to me, 'You shall not build a house for
My name, because you are a man of war and have shed
blood.' ... He said to me, 'Your son Solomon is the one who
shall build My house.'"

—1 Chronicles 28:2–3, 28:6 *(NASB)*

How do we respond when we realize we will never accomplish that one thing we always wanted to? As much as we had
our heart set on it, we won't see that day come, or we won't
achieve that mark. Well, if we realize we're not just in a race,
but in a relay, we will find contentment in letting the Lord
use us to set up the next generation, like David did with Solomon and God's temple.

Then King David turned to the entire assembly and said, "My son Solomon, whom God has clearly chosen as the next king of Israel, is still young and inexperienced. The work ahead of him is enormous, for the Temple he will build is not for mere mortals—it is for the LORD God himself! ... And now, because of my devotion to the Temple of my God, I am giving all of my own private treasures of gold and silver to help in the construction."

—1 Chronicles 29:1, 29:3

Legacy people understand sacrifice. They choose to do less for themselves so they can do more for others.

David said, "I won't see the temple in my lifetime, but I'm not living for my lifetime. I'm living for eternity." In a season of life when so many people filter their existence through the lens of a ticking clock—thinking about much more they can get, do, enjoy, and experience before it's all suddenly over—David was not consumed by the rising and setting of the sun. He was driven by eternity.

Legacy people understand sacrifice. They choose to do less for themselves so they can do more for others. Here was David, in front of all the leaders of Israel, telling his son to take courage and be a man. David wanted Solomon to give his whole heart and service willingly to God, so he gave sacrificially of his own resources for the work that Solomon would do in building the temple.

Legacy people also live with a sense an urgency.

No wonder Solomon later asked for wisdom when God

told him, "I'll give you anything you ask for" (2 Chronicles 1). Solomon didn't ask for money or fame, but for wisdom to lead God's people wisely. Like David, his father, Solomon wasn't perfect, yet he became the wisest and wealthiest person in the world. It's the wisdom of God that brings the wealth—and with wisdom, instead of the wealth owning us, we own the wealth. In Jesus' words:

> Do not store up for yourselves treasures on earth, where moths and vermin destroy, and where thieves break in and steal. But store up for yourselves treasures in heaven, where moths and vermin do not destroy, and where thieves do not break in and steal.
> **—Matthew 6:19-20**

Let's decide that more than anything else, we want to know God's heart and lead our life with the wisdom and understanding that come from Him. As men leaving legacies, let's choose a life of sacrifice, storing up treasures in heaven, the way David modeled for us. Success is determined by what we're willing to give up.

Living with Urgency

Legacy people also live with a sense an urgency. If you want to be a man with a legacy—and I think you do, because God has placed that desire in the heart of every man—then do something about it *today*. Encourage someone today. Serve someone today. Make a difference *today*. Learn to number your days, the way David did, by making every day count.

> *Then he continued, "Be strong and courageous and get to work."*
> **—1 Chronicles 28:20** *(TLB)*

Don't be frightened with what God has called you to do. Get to work! I know it's scary to pick up that baton and deal with the addiction in your family, with your anger, or with your trust and abandonment issues. But pick up that baton, anyway, and *get to work!* Don't be frightened by the size of the task, for the Lord your God is with you, and He will not forsake you. He will see to it that everything is finished correctly.

"Well," we might say, "someday I'll..." No—stop putting off the important things for "someday" and start living *today*. Get to work! In the New Testament, we find that Paul said as much to Timothy, about the work of preaching the gospel:

> *I urge you, Timothy, as we live in the sight of God and of Christ Jesus (whose coming in power will judge the living and the dead), to preach the Word of God. Never lose your sense of urgency, in season or out of season.*
> **—2 Timothy 4:1–2** *(PHILLIPS)*

Legacy is not a "someday" thing; it's an accumulation of everyday little things, in every season. And take note: young men don't have to wait until they're old sages, like Paul, to begin leaving a legacy. Like Timothy, men of every age can make a difference, too, *today* and every day. We have to live carefully and make the most of every opportunity, on a daily basis, never knowing which day on this earth will be our last:

> *Be very careful, then, how you live—not as unwise but as wise, making the most of every opportunity, because the days are evil.*
>
> **—Ephesians 5:15–16**

WRITING A NEW LEGACY

Alfred woke up one day and read his name in the obituary column.

You see, his brother had died a week prior, and the newspaper got the names mixed up. Not only that, but to Alfred's chagrin, the obituary slapped him with a label based on his legacy at the time: "Alfred Nobel, Merchant of Death." Alfred Nobel was best known for inventing dynamite, but he also helped develop military explosives—hence, the unsavory epithet, "Merchant of Death."[22]

Instead of suing the paper, Alfred acknowledged the obituary was right and decided he was going to spend the remaining years of his life changing his legacy. Rather than be forever known as the Merchant of Death, he wanted to be remembered as someone who brought peace and benefit to humankind. Using the profits from his inventions, he established the annual Nobel Prizes, including the Nobel Peace Prize, to recognize individuals from around the world who made the greatest contributions in different areas. Today, we remember him for the Nobel Peace Prize more than for his scientific achievements or deadly inventions.

Alfred Nobel changed his legacy, and so can you. Maybe you're known as the man who holds grudges, the man who's stingy with his money, or the man who has a temper. The good news is, your legacy doesn't start when you die; it starts today. There's time to rewrite your obituary!

Remember how the book of Acts describes the end of David's long life as a man after God's own heart:

> *Now when David had served God's purpose in his own generation, he fell asleep.*
>
> *—Acts 13:36*

"Now when [insert your name here] had served God's purpose in his own generation, he fell asleep." How does that sound to you? To me, it sounds like being a man of legacy.

Now, choose to begin writing a new legacy for yourself today. Man up, pick up that baton, and get to work!

Chapter Seven Questions

Question: What will you leave when you leave? Include the good and the bad aspects of your current legacy. What legacy has the Lord put on your heart to leave?

_____

_____

_____

_____

_____

_____

_____

_____

Question: Do you have an eternal mindset? How, specifically, can you demonstrate that you've adopted this kind of legacy-minded perspective?

_____

_____

_____

_____

_____

_____

_____

_____

Question: How can you live with a greater sense of urgency, while still trusting God more than your own strength and skill?

_____

_____

_____

_____

_____

_____

_____

_____

_____

_____

_____

_____

Action: Write an obituary for yourself that captures the heart of the legacy you want to leave. Identify your next step toward making that legacy a reality. Then, man up and take that step!

Chapter Seven Notes

_____

_____

_____

_____

_____

_____

_____

_____

_____

_____

_____

_____

_____

_____

_____

What You Were Called to Be

Here, as this book comes to a close, I will repeat this declaration by John Eldredge I quoted in the introduction: *"A boy becomes a man only through the active intervention of his father and the fellowship of men. It cannot happen any other way."*

Because this is true, it is crucial for men to grow into God-approved masculinity as fathers to the next generation and as brothers to each other. Even more crucial is recognizing and leaning into the truth that only our Father can develop our soul and make each of us a finished man. The Father accomplishes this through Jesus when we place our trust in Him.

As we've discovered, a man's relationship with God looks different at different times over the course of his life. What stage or stages of masculinity are you at right now?

Are you still lingering in the boy or cowboy stage?

Are you a young man exploring what it means to be a warrior or a lover?

Are you trying to step into roles of leadership as a king?

Are you ready to serve as a sage, helping to raise up the next generation in wisdom and truth?

Wherever you are in your journey to becoming a man, I know you face challenges, temptations, and struggles. It's inevitable. This is why, in every stage of life, a man needs to be in a personal relationship with God—learning to love, trust, and obey Him—to become who he was made to be.

Our Father has called us to follow Jesus as our perfect example, yet we don't have to be perfect now, in the past, or in the future. Jesus takes care of our flaws and imperfections. He makes us finished men in the places where our past and our shortcomings have left us unfinished.

So above all, have a heart for God and, in turn, be a man after His heart. Be a warrior, lover, king, and sage in the mold of your heavenly Father and His Son, Jesus. Let His Holy Spirit shape every aspect of your life and character. Do less for yourself and more for others. Encourage, serve, and teach. Recapture the heart of manhood as a father—in your family and in your church family. From this day forward, choose a legacy of strength, courage, and commitment. Choose to man up!

About the Author

Jason Hanash is the founding pastor of Discovery Church, which is one of the fastest-growing churches in America due to his powerful and practical preaching and leadership development. He is also on the Lead Team with Church Boom, a coaching ministry for pastors and church leaders. Jason is a speaker, author, church planters' coach, pastors' coach, and leadership coach.

About Renown Publishing

Renown Publishing was founded with one mission in mind: to make your great idea famous.

At Renown Publishing, we don't just publish. We work hard to pair strategy with innovative marketing techniques so that your book launch is the start of something bigger.

Learn more at RenownPublishing.com.

REFERENCES

Notes

1. Eldredge, John. *Fathered by God*. Thomas Nelson, 2009.

2. Based on a search for "David" in the New Living Translation of the Bible (NLT) using Bible Gateway: https://www.biblegateway.com/quicksearch/?quicksearch=David&version=NLT.

3. Myers, Jeremy. "Did David's Mother Commit Adultery?" Redeeming God. https://redeeminggod.com/davids-mother-commit-adultery/.

4. Josephus, Flavius. *Antiquities of the Jews* 6.8.1. https://penelope.uchicago.edu/josephus/ant-6.html.

5. A similar saying is commonly attributed both to the seventeenth-century English preacher and author John Bunyan and to the nineteenth-century American evangelist D. L. Moody.

6. Chapman, David. *The Power of Praise: The 7 Hebrew Words for Praise.* TRU, 2014.

7. Chapman, *The Power of Praise.*

8. Chapman, *The Power of Praise.*

9. Chapman, *The Power of Praise.*

10. Chapman, *The Power of Praise.*

11. Chapman, *The Power of Praise.*

12. Chapman, *The Power of Praise.*

13. Bonhoeffer, Dietrich. *Temptation.* SCM Press, 1961, p. 33. Quoted in Tim Campbell, "Temptation (Bonhoeffer)." Faithlife Sermons. https://sermons.faithlife.com/sermons/84110-temptation-(bonhoeffer).

14. Owen, John. *Of the Mortification of Sin in Believers.* Ch. 2. Christian Classics Ethereal Library. https://ccel.org/ccel/owen/mort/mort.i.v.html.

15. Pulver, Jens, and Erich Krauss. *Little Evil.* ECW, 2003.

16 . Livingston, Gretchen. "About One-Third of U. S. Children Are Living with an Unmarried Parent." Pew Research Center. April 27, 2018. https://www.pewresearch.org/fact-tank/2018/04/27/about-one-third-of-u-s-children-are-living-with-an-unmarried-parent/.

17. Makou, Gopolang. "Analysis: Mistakes About Madiba — Even by Himself." Africa Check. December 4, 2016. https://africacheck.org/fact-checks/blog/analysis-mistakes-about-madiba-even-himself.

18. Blue Letter Bible, "Strong's H2654 – ḥāpēṣ." https://www. blueletterbible.org/lexicon/h2654/kjv/wlc/0-1/.

19. *Brown-Driver-Briggs Lexicon*, "Strong's H8003." In Blue Letter Bible, "Strong's H8003 – šālēm." https://www.blueletter bible.org/lexicon/h8003/kjv/wlc/0-1/.

20. Stat, Terri Yablonsky. "Be Generous: It's a Simple Way to Stay Healthier." Chicago Tribune. August 6, 2015. https://www.chicagotribune.com/lifestyles/health/sc-hlth-0812-joy-of-giving-20150806-story.html.

21. Koltko-Rivera, Mark E. "Rediscovering the Later Version of Maslow's Hierarchy of Needs: Self-Transendence and Opportunities for Theory, Research, and Unification." *Review of General Psychology* 10, no. 4 (December 1, 2006). https://doi.org/10.1037%2F1089-2680.10.4.302.

22. Golden, Frederic. "The Worst and the Brightest." Time. October 16, 2000.

Made in the USA
Las Vegas, NV
13 June 2022